ME[illegible]NEAN
COUNTRY KITCHEN

MEDITERRANEAN
COUNTRY COOKING

MEDITERRANEAN STYLE CAPTURED IN
SIMPLY STUNNING DISHES

Jacqueline Clark and Joanna Farrow

HERMES HOUSE

This edition published by Hermes House
an imprint of
Anness Publishing Limited
Hermes House, 88–89 Blackfriars Road, London SE1 8HA

A CIP catalogue record for this book is available from the British Library.

Publisher: Joanna Lorenz
Senior Cookery Editor: Linda Fraser
Editor: Margaret Malone
Designer: Nigel Partridge
Jacket Design: Balley Design Associates
Photography and styling: Michelle Garrett, assisted by Dulce Riberio
Food for photography: Jacqueline Clark and Joanna Farrow
Illustrator: Anna Koska
Front cover: Nicki Dowey, Photographer and Stylist;
Angela Boggiano, Home Economist

Previously published as part of a larger compendium, *A Taste of the Mediterranean*

Printed in China
1 3 5 7 9 10 8 6 4 2

NOTES

For all recipes, quantities are given in both metric and imperial measures and, where appropriate, measures are also given in standard cups and spoons. Follow one set, but not a mixture because they are not interchangeable.

Standard spoon and cup measures are level.
1 tsp = 5ml, 1 tbsp = 15ml, 1 cup = 250ml/8 fl oz

Medium eggs should be used unless otherwise stated.

CONTENTS

INTRODUCTION

Today, fresh vegetables, fruits, herbs, spices, pulses and grains, feature as strongly in country Mediterranean cooking as they have for hundreds of years. Recent research has shown the Mediterranean diet to be a very healthy one, and a large part of its success is due to this insistence on using fresh seasonal ingredients. In every region, ingredients are bought daily from the local market to produce classic time-honoured dishes.

In cooking everywhere, not just in the Mediterranean countryside, the seasons should be reflected in any choice of dishes. A country cook prefers to use produce that is in season and is at its freshest and best. Mediterranean products, such as tomatoes, aubergines, courgettes, peaches, garlic, figs, grains, nuts and pulses, are increasingly found in dishes all over the world but are not always used to their full advantage.

From hearty soups to aromatic main dishes, *Country Mediterranean Cooking* draws on traditional country heritage to provide over 50 authentic recipes, each one demonstrating the wonderful results that can be achieved with the right ingredients in the right combination. The book is divided into six chapters: Starters and Soups; Vegetables and Salads; Fish and Seafood; Meat, Poultry and Game; Breads and Grains; and Desserts and Pastries. All the recipes have been specially chosen to highlight traditional flavours and textures and also to reflect the impact of the changing seasons on country cooking. For example, the hearty slow-cooked stew Provençal Beef and Olive Daube, is perfect for long, cold winter nights, while Tapenade and Herb Aïoli with Summer Vegetables, and Italian Prawn Skewers, are ideal for summer meals *al fresco*. Of course some dishes – such as Lemon Tart and Stuffed Peaches with Mascarpone Cream – deserve to be eaten all year round.

This book contains a wonderful collection of recipes that give a flavour of Mediterranean cooking. With an information-packed introduction full of facts about fresh and store cupboard ingredients, a simple step-by-step format with helpful cook's tips and glorious full-colour photographs of every dish, this evocative book is the essential guide to country Mediterranean cooking and will ensure that whatever the occasion, even the novice cook can be sure of bringing to the table an authentic, delicious taste of the Mediterranean.

Artichokes

Fennel

Ingredients

Okra

Vegetables

ARTICHOKES When buying, choose firm, taut specimens. After boiling, the leaves and base are edible.

AUBERGINES Firm, taut, shiny-skinned with green stalks, aubergines are sometimes salted and drained before cooking, which helps to extract bitter juices and makes them absorb less oil during cooking.

COURGETTES At their best when they are small, they can be eaten raw, and have a good flavour and crisp texture. The larger they become, the less flavour they have.

MUSHROOMS The varieties most often used are button, open cup and flat, but regional wild species such as ceps and oyster mushrooms are also used.

ONIONS When the onion is to be used raw, choose red or white-skinned varieties, which have a sweet, mild flavour. Baby onions are perfect for adding whole to stews, or serving as a vegetable dish on their own.

PEPPERS To make the most of their flavour, grill peppers until the skins are charred, then rub off and discard the skins. Marinate the peppers in olive oil.

SPINACH Young spinach leaves can be eaten raw and need little preparation, but older leaves should be picked over carefully and the tough stalks removed.

TOMATOES Full of flavour, tomatoes come in many varieties – plum tomatoes, beef-steak tomatoes, vine tomatoes, cherry tomatoes and baby pear-shaped ones.

Olives

Fresh olives are picked at the desired stage of ripeness, then soaked in water, bruised and immersed in brine to produce the familiar-tasting result. They can be bought whole or pitted, sometimes stuffed with peppers, or nuts, or bottled with flavourings such as garlic, chilli and herbs.

Dairy Produce

CHEESE The range of cheese from Mediterranean countries is diverse – varieties are made from cow's, goat's, ewe's and even buffalo's milk.

YOGURT Used in dips, marinades and to enrich soups and stews, it is made from goat's, ewe's or cow's milk.

Grains

COUSCOUS This is a product made from semolina. The commercial variety simply needs moistening, then steaming to swell the grains and produce a soft texture. It is usually served with a spicy meat or vegetable stew,

Radishes

but it can also be used as a stuffing or in salads.

RICE There are many varieties of this world-wide staple food. In Italy there are at least four short-grained types used in risottos alone, and in Spain, Valencia rice is the preferred variety for paella.

Vine tomatoes

FRUIT

DATES Fresh dates should be plump and slightly wrinkled and have a rich honey-like flavour and dense texture. They are best treated simply, or stoned and served with thick Greek yogurt.

FIGS Colour may vary from purple to golden yellow, but all are made up of hundreds of tiny seeds, surrounded by soft pink flesh which is perfectly edible. Choose firm unblemished fruit, which just yield to the touch.

PEACHES AND NECTARINES Peaches need plenty of sun to ripen them and there are yellow, pink and white-fleshed varieties. Look for bruise-free specimens that just give when squeezed gently. Nectarines are smooth-skinned, with all the luscious flavour of the peach.

FISH AND SHELLFISH

MUSSELS Open mussels should be discarded if they do not close after a sharp tap. They are easy to cook – just steam for a few minutes in a pan.

PRAWNS These vary enormously in size. The classic Mediterranean prawn is large, about 20cm/8in, reddish brown in colour when raw, and pink when cooked.

SQUID These vary in size, from tiny specimens that can be eaten whole, to larger varieties, which are good for stuffing, grilling or stewing.

TUNA Keep the flesh moist by marinating before cooking, or by basting while cooking. Tuna can be baked, fried, grilled or stewed.

PULSES

CHICK-PEAS Often used in stews, this pulse looks like a pale golden hazelnut and has a mild, nutty flavour.

HARICOT BEANS These small plump white beans need to be soaked for 3–4 hours before cooking, and are good in casseroles, soups and salads.

LENTILS These come in different sizes and can be yellow, red, brown or green. They are used mostly in soups and need no soaking time, cooking in under an hour.

PASTA

In Italy today there are countless varieties, from flat sheets of lasagne and ribbon noodles to pressed and moulded shapes. Dried pasta shapes make a good standby, but fresh has a better flavour and texture and freezes well.

NUTS

ALMONDS These are an important ingredient in sweet pastries and are often added to savoury dishes, too.

WALNUTS This very versatile nut is used in both sweet and savoury dishes. Walnuts are chopped and added to pastries, ground to make sauces, or eaten fresh.

HERBS

BASIL One of the herbs most crucial to Mediterranean cooking. The sweet tender leaves are delicious with tomatoes, aubergines, peppers, courgettes and cheese.

BAY Widely used to flavour slow-cooked recipes like stocks, soups and stews, it is also added to marinades, threaded on to kebab skewers or thrown on the barbecue to invigorate the smoky taste.

CORIANDER The leaves impart a distinctive flavour to soups, stews, sauces and spicy dishes when added towards the end of cooking.

MINT One of the oldest and most widely used herbs.

Finely chopped mint adds a cooling tang to yogurt dishes as well as teas and iced drinks.

ROSEMARY Widely used in meat cookery, several sprigs, tucked under a roast chicken or lamb with plenty of garlic, impart a warm, sweet flavour.

THYME A few sprigs of hardy thyme add a warm, earthy flavour to slow-cooked meat and poultry dishes as well as to pâtés, marinades and vegetable dishes.

SPICES

CHILLIES Mediterranean chillies are generally milder in flavour than the unbearably fiery South American ones but should still be used with caution as their heat is difficult to gauge.

CINNAMON Cinnamon sticks have an aromatic, sweet flavour that is used to enhance meat and *pilau* dishes, and to infuse milk and syrups for puddings.

CORIANDER SEEDS The seeds of the coriander herb have a warm, slightly orange aroma which can be accentuated by crushing and gently heating the seeds in a frying pan before using.

CUMIN SEEDS These dark, spindly shaped seeds are often married with coriander when making spicy dishes.

Figs

Sea bass

NUTMEG Nutmeg's beautiful, sweet warm aroma makes a good addition to sweet and savoury dishes.

PEPPER There are several different types of peppercorns: black peppercorns have the strongest flavour, while green peppercorns are the fresh unripe berries which are bottled while soft.

SAFFRON Its exotic, rich colour and flavour is indispensable in many Mediterranean dishes. To accentuate the taste the strands are best lightly crushed and soaked in a little boiling water before use.

FLAVOURINGS

CAPERS The sharp piquant tang of capers is used to cut the richness of lamb, enliven fish sauces and flavour salads and pastes such as *tapenade*.

GARLIC Sold in "strings" or as separate bulbs, when buying garlic ensure that the cloves are plump and firm. Use crushed, sliced or even whole.

LEMONS AND LIMES The grated rind or squeezed juice of lemons and limes are widely added to fish, meat and poultry for a typically fresh flavour.

TAHINI A smooth oily paste ground from sesame seeds and used to give a nutty flavour to Middle Eastern dishes.

OLIVE OIL

Besides its healthy qualities, olive oil is indispensable to Mediterranean cooking for its fine, nutty flavour. The richest oil comes from the first cold pressing of the olives, producing a deep green "virgin" oil.

STARTERS AND SOUPS

An irresistible choice of textures and flavours.

DEEP FRIED NEW POTATOES WITH SAFFRON AÏOLI

Aïoli is a Spanish garlic mayonnaise, similar to the French mayonnaise of the same name. In this recipe saffron adds colour and flavour.

1 size 2 egg yolk
2.5ml/½ tsp Dijon mustard
300ml/½ pint/1¼ cups extra virgin olive oil
15–30ml/1–2 tbsp lemon juice
1 garlic clove, crushed
2.5ml/½ tsp saffron strands
20 baby new potatoes
vegetable oil for frying
salt and ground black pepper

SERVES 4

1 To make the aïoli, put the egg yolk in a bowl with the mustard and a pinch of salt. Beat together with a wooden spoon. Still beating, add the olive oil very slowly, drop by drop to begin with, then, as the aïoli gradually thickens, in a thin stream. Add the lemon juice and salt and pepper to taste, then beat in the crushed garlic.

2 Place the saffron in a small bowl, and add 10ml/2 tsp hot water. Press the saffron with the back of a teaspoon, to extract the colour and flavour, and leave to infuse for 5 minutes. Beat the saffron and the liquid into the mayonnaise.

3 Cook the potatoes in boiling salted water for 5 minutes, then turn off the heat. Cover the pan and leave for 15 minutes. Drain the potatoes, then dry them thoroughly.

4 Heat 1cm/½ in oil in a deep pan. When the oil is very hot, add the potatoes, and fry quickly, turning, until crisp and golden. Drain on kitchen paper, and serve with the saffron aïoli.

DATES STUFFED WITH CHORIZO

A delicious combination from Spain, using fresh dates and spicy chorizo sausage.

50g/2oz chorizo sausage
12 fresh dates, stoned
6 streaky bacon rashers
oil for frying
plain flour for dusting
1 egg, beaten
50g/2oz/1 cup fresh breadcrumbs
cocktail sticks for serving

SERVES 4–6

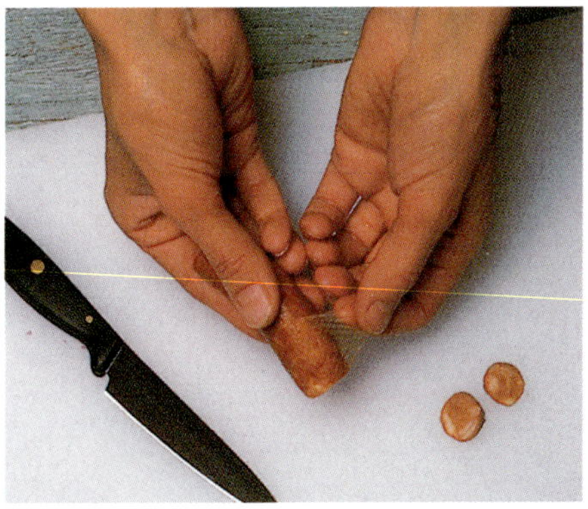

1 Trim the ends of the chorizo sausage and peel away the skin. Cut into three 2cm/¾in slices. Cut these in half lengthways, then into quarters, giving 12 pieces.

2 Stuff each date with a piece of chorizo, closing the date around it. Stretch the bacon, by running the back of a knife along the rasher. Cut each rasher in half, widthways. Wrap a piece of bacon around each date and secure with a cocktail stick.

3 In a deep pan, heat 1cm/½in of oil. Dust the dates with flour, dip them in the beaten egg, then coat in breadcrumbs. Fry the dates in the hot oil, turning them, until golden. Remove the dates with a slotted spoon, and drain on kitchen paper. Serve immediately.

VINICOLA
HIDALGO

Tapas of Almonds, Olives and Cheese

These three simple ingredients are lightly flavoured to create a delicious Spanish tapas medley that's perfect for a casual starter or nibbles to serve with pre-dinner drinks.

For the marinated olives
2.5ml/½ tsp coriander seeds
2.5ml/½ tsp fennel seeds
5ml/1 tsp chopped fresh rosemary
10ml/2 tsp chopped fresh parsley
2 garlic cloves, crushed
15ml/1 tbsp sherry vinegar
30ml/2 tbsp olive oil
115g/4oz/⅔ cup black olives
115g/4oz/⅔ cup green olives

For the marinated cheese
150g/5oz goat's cheese, preferably manchego
90ml/6 tbsp olive oil
15ml/1 tbsp white wine vinegar
5ml/1 tsp black peppercorns
1 garlic clove, sliced
3 fresh tarragon or thyme sprigs
tarragon sprigs, to garnish

For the salted almonds
1.5ml/¼ tsp cayenne pepper
30ml/2 tbsp sea salt
25g/1oz/2 tbsp butter
60ml/4 tbsp olive oil
200g/7oz/1¾ cups blanched almonds
extra salt for sprinkling (optional)

Serves 6–8

1 To make the marinated olives, crush the coriander and fennel seeds with a pestle and mortar. Mix together with the rosemary, parsley, garlic, vinegar and oil and pour over the olives in a small bowl. Cover and chill for up to 1 week.

2 To make the marinated cheese, cut the cheese into bite-size pieces, leaving the rind on. Mix together the oil, vinegar, peppercorns, garlic and herb sprigs and pour over the cheese in a small bowl. Cover and chill for up to 3 days.

3 To make the salted almonds, mix together the cayenne pepper and salt in a bowl. Melt the butter with the olive oil in a frying pan. Add the almonds to the pan and fry, stirring for about 5 minutes, until the almonds are golden.

4 Tip the almonds out of the frying pan, into the salt mixture and toss together until the almonds are coated. Leave to cool, then store them in a jar or airtight container for up to 1 week.

5 To serve the tapas, arrange in small, shallow serving dishes. Use fresh sprigs of tarragon to garnish the cheese and scatter the almonds with a little more salt, if liked.

Cook's Tip

If serving with pre-dinner drinks, provide cocktail sticks for spearing the olives and cheese.

GARLIC PRAWNS

For this simple Spanish tapas dish, you really need fresh raw prawns which absorb the flavours of the garlic and chilli as they fry. Have everything ready for last minute cooking so you can take it to the table still sizzling.

350–450g/12oz–1lb large raw prawns
2 red chillies
75ml/5 tbsp olive oil
3 garlic cloves, crushed
salt and ground black pepper

SERVES 4

1 Remove the heads and shells from the prawns, leaving the tails intact.

2 Halve each chilli lengthways and discard the seeds. Heat the oil in a flameproof pan, suitable for serving. (Alternatively, use a frying pan and have a warmed serving dish ready in the oven.)

3 Add all the prawns, chilli and garlic to the pan and cook over a high heat for about 3 minutes, stirring until the prawns turn pink. Season lightly with salt and pepper and serve immediately.

CHORIZO IN OLIVE OIL

Spanish chorizo sausage has a deliciously pungent taste; its robust seasoning of garlic, chilli and paprika flavours the ingredients it is cooked with. Frying chorizo with onions and olive oil is one of its simplest and most delicious uses.

75ml/5 tbsp extra virgin olive oil
350g/12oz chorizo sausage, sliced
1 large onion, thinly sliced
roughly chopped flat leaf parsley, to garnish

SERVES 4

1 Heat the oil in a frying pan and fry the chorizo sausage over a high heat until beginning to colour. Remove from pan with slotted spoon.

2 Add the onion to the pan and fry until coloured. Return the sausage slices to the pan and heat through for 1 minute.

3 Tip the mixture into a shallow serving dish and scatter with the parsley. Serve with warm bread.

VARIATION

Chorizo is usually available in large supermarkets or delicatessens. Other similarly rich, spicy sausages can be used as a substitute.

BRANDADE DE MORUE

Salt cod is popular in Spain and France and it can be found cooked in a number of ways. This recipe is a purée, flavoured with garlic and olive oil, which is made all over southern France.

675g/1½lb salt cod
300ml/½ pint/1¼ cups olive oil
250ml/8fl oz/1 cup milk
1 garlic clove, crushed
grated nutmeg
lemon juice, to taste
white pepper

For the croutes
50ml/2fl oz/¼ cup olive oil
6 slices white bread, crusts removed
1 garlic clove, halved
parsley sprigs, to garnish

Serves 6

1 Soak the salt cod in cold water for at least 24 hours, changing the water several times. Drain.

2 To make the croûtes, heat the oil in a frying pan. Cut the bread slices in half diagonally and fry in the oil until golden. Drain on kitchen paper, then rub on both sides with garlic.

3 Put the cod in a large pan, with enough cold water to cover. Cover and bring to the boil. Simmer gently for 8–10 minutes, until just tender. Drain and cool. Flake the fish and discard any skin and bone.

4 Heat the oil in a pan until very hot. In a separate pan, scald the milk. Transfer the fish to a blender or food processor and, with the motor running, slowly pour in the hot oil, followed by the milk, until the mixture is smooth and stiff. Transfer to a bowl and beat in the crushed garlic. Season with nutmeg, lemon juice and white pepper. Leave the *brandade* to cool and then chill until almost ready to serve.

5 Spoon the *brandade* into a shallow serving bowl and surround with the croûtes. Garnish with parsley and serve cold.

SPICY PUMPKIN SOUP

Pumpkin is popular all over the Mediterranean and it's an important ingredient in Middle Eastern cookery, from which this soup is inspired. Ginger and cumin give the soup its spicy flavour.

900g/2lb pumpkin, peeled and seeds removed
30ml/2 tbsp olive oil
2 leeks, trimmed and sliced
1 garlic clove, crushed
5ml/1 tsp ground ginger
5ml/1 tsp ground cumin
900ml/1½ pints/3¾ cups chicken stock
salt and ground black pepper
coriander leaves, to garnish
60ml/4 tbsp natural yogurt, to serve

SERVES 4

1 Cut the pumpkin into chunks. Heat the oil in a large pan and add the leeks and garlic. Cook gently until softened.

2 Add the ginger and cumin and cook, stirring, for a further minute. Add the pumpkin and the chicken stock and season with salt and pepper. Bring to the boil and simmer for 30 minutes, until the pumpkin is tender. Process the soup, in batches if necessary, in a blender or food processor.

3 Reheat the soup and serve in warmed individual bowls, with a swirl of yogurt and a garnish of coriander leaves.

BOUILLABAISSE

Perhaps the most famous of all Mediterranean fish soups, this recipe, originating from Marseilles in the south of France, is a rich and colourful mixture of fish and shellfish, flavoured with tomatoes, saffron and orange.

1.5kg/3–3½lb mixed fish and raw shellfish, such as red mullet, John Dory, monkfish, red snapper, whiting, large prawns and clams
225g/8oz well-flavoured tomatoes
pinch of saffron strands
90ml/6 tbsp olive oil
1 onion, sliced
1 leek, sliced
1 celery stick, sliced
2 garlic cloves, crushed
1 bouquet garni
1 strip pared orange rind
2.5ml/½ tsp fennel seeds
salt and ground black pepper
15ml/1 tbsp tomato purée
10ml/2 tsp Pernod
4–6 thick slices French bread
45ml/3 tbsp chopped fresh parsley

SERVES 4–6

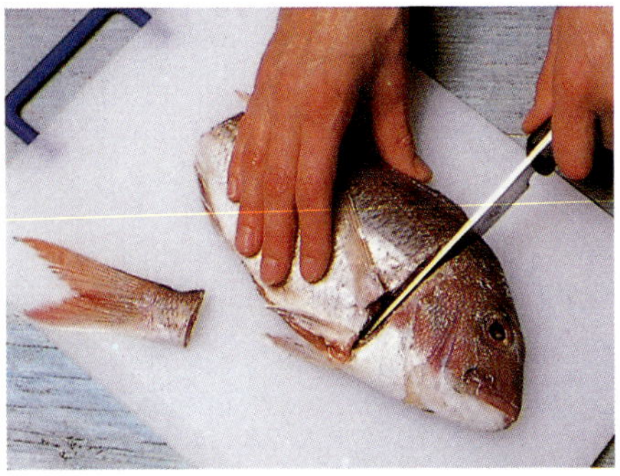

1 Remove the heads, tails and fins from the fish and put them in a large pan, with 1.2 litres/2 pints/5 cups water. Bring to the boil, and simmer for 15 minutes. Strain, and reserve the liquid.

2 Cut the fish into large chunks. Leave the shellfish in their shells. Scald the tomatoes, then drain and refresh in cold water. Peel and roughly chop them. Soak the saffron in 15–30ml/1–2 tbsp hot water.

3 Heat the oil in a large pan, add the onion, leek and celery and cook until softened. Add the garlic, bouquet garni, orange rind, fennel seeds and tomatoes, then stir in the saffron and liquid and the fish stock. Season with salt and pepper, then bring to the boil and simmer for 30–40 minutes.

4 Add the shellfish and boil for about 6 minutes. Add the fish and cook for a further 6–8 minutes, until it flakes easily.

5 Using a slotted spoon, transfer the fish to a warmed serving platter. Keep the liquid boiling, to allow the oil to emulsify with the broth. Add the tomato purée and Pernod, then check the seasoning. To serve, place a slice of French bread in each soup bowl, pour the broth over the top and serve the fish separately, sprinkled with the parsley.

SPICED MUSSEL SOUP

Chunky and colourful, this Turkish fish soup is like a chowder in its consistency. It's flavoured with harissa sauce, more familiar in North African cookery.

1.5kg/3–3½lb fresh mussels
150ml/¼ pint/⅔ cup white wine
3 tomatoes
30ml/2 tbsp olive oil
1 onion, finely chopped
2 garlic cloves, crushed
2 celery sticks, thinly sliced
bunch of spring onions, thinly sliced
1 potato, diced
7.5ml/1½ tsp harissa sauce
45ml/3 tbsp chopped fresh parsley
ground black pepper
thick yogurt, to serve (optional)

SERVES 6

1 Scrub the mussels, discarding any damaged ones or any open ones that do not close when tapped with a knife.

2 Bring the wine to the boil in a large saucepan. Add the mussels and cover with a lid. Cook for 4–5 minutes until the mussels have opened wide. Discard any mussels that remain closed. Drain the mussels, reserving the cooking liquid. Reserve a few mussels in their shells for garnish and shell the rest.

3 Peel the tomatoes and dice them. Heat the oil in a pan and fry the onion, garlic, celery and spring onions for 5 minutes.

4 Add the shelled mussels, reserved liquid, potato, harissa sauce and tomatoes. Bring just to the boil, reduce the heat and cover. Simmer gently for 25 minutes, or until the potatoes are breaking up.

5 Stir in the parsley and pepper and add the reserved mussels. Heat through for 1 minute. Serve hot with a spoonful of yogurt, if you like.

GREEN LENTIL SOUP

Lentil soup is an Eastern Mediterranean classic, varying in its spiciness according to region. Red or puy lentils make an equally good substitute for the green lentils used here.

225g/8oz/1 cup green lentils
75ml/5 tbsp olive oil
3 onions, finely chopped
2 garlic cloves, thinly sliced
10ml/2 tsp cumin seeds, crushed
1.5ml/¼ tsp ground turmeric
600ml/1 pint/2½ cups chicken or vegetable stock
salt and ground black pepper
30ml/2 tbsp roughly chopped fresh coriander, to finish

SERVES 4–6

1 Put the lentils in a saucepan and cover with cold water. Bring to the boil and boil rapidly for 10 minutes. Drain.

2 Heat 30ml/2 tbsp of the oil in a pan and fry two of the onions with the garlic, cumin and turmeric for 3 minutes, stirring. Add the lentils, stock and 600ml/1 pint/2½ cups water. Bring to the boil, reduce the heat, cover and simmer gently for 30 minutes, until the lentils are soft.

3 Fry the third onion in the remaining oil until golden.

4 Use a potato masher to lightly mash the lentils and make the soup pulpy. Reheat gently and season with salt and pepper to taste. Pour the soup into bowls. Stir the fresh coriander into the fried onion and scatter over the soup. Serve with warm bread.

MOROCCAN HARIRA

This is a hearty meat and vegetable soup, eaten during the month of Ramadan, when the Muslim population fast between sunrise and sunset.

450g/1lb well-flavoured tomatoes
225g/8oz lamb, cut into 1cm/½in pieces
2.5ml/½ tsp ground turmeric
2.5ml/½ tsp ground cinnamon
25g/1oz/2 tbsp butter
60ml/4 tbsp chopped fresh coriander
30ml/2 tbsp chopped fresh parsley
1 onion, chopped
50g/2oz/¼ cup split red lentils
75g/3oz/½ cup dried chick-peas, soaked overnight
4 baby onions or small shallots, peeled
25g/1oz/¼ cup soup noodles
salt and ground black pepper
chopped fresh coriander, lemon slices and ground cinnamon, to garnish

SERVES 4

1 Plunge the tomatoes into boiling water for 30 seconds, then refresh in cold water. Peel away the skins. Cut into quarters and remove the seeds. Chop roughly.

2 Put the lamb, turmeric, cinnamon, butter, coriander, parsley and onion into a large pan, and cook over a moderate heat, stirring, for 5 minutes. Add the chopped tomatoes and continue to cook for 10 minutes.

3 Rinse the lentils under running water and add to the pan with the drained chick-peas and 600ml/1 pint/2½ cups water. Season with salt and pepper. Bring to the boil, cover, and simmer gently for 1½ hours.

4 Add the baby onions and cook for a further 30 minutes. Add the noodles 5 minutes before the end of this cooking time. Garnish with the coriander, lemon slices and cinnamon.

GALICIAN BROTH

This delicious main meal soup is very similar to the warming, chunky meat and potato broths of cooler climates. For extra colour, a few onion skins can be added when cooking the gammon, but remember to remove them before serving.

450g/1lb gammon, in one piece
2 bay leaves
2 onions, sliced
10ml/2 tsp paprika
675g/1½lb potatoes, cut into large chunks
225g/8oz spring greens
425g/15oz can haricot or cannellini beans, drained
salt and ground black pepper

SERVES 4

1 Soak the gammon overnight in cold water. Drain and put in a large saucepan with the bay leaves and onions. Pour over 1.5 litres/ 2½ pints/6¼ cups cold water.

2 Bring to the boil then reduce the heat and simmer very gently for about 1½ hours until the meat is tender. Keep an eye on the pan to make sure it doesn't boil over.

3 Drain the meat, reserving the cooking liquid and leave to cool slightly. Discard the skin and any excess fat from the meat and cut into small chunks. Return to the pan with the paprika and potatoes. Cover and simmer gently for 20 minutes.

4 Cut away the cores from the greens. Roll up the leaves and cut into thin shreds. Add to the pan with the beans and simmer for about 10 minutes. Season with salt and pepper to taste and serve hot.

COOK'S TIP

Bacon knuckles can be used instead of the gammon. The bones will give the juices a delicious flavour.

VEGETABLES AND SALADS

A veritable treasure trove of taste and colour.

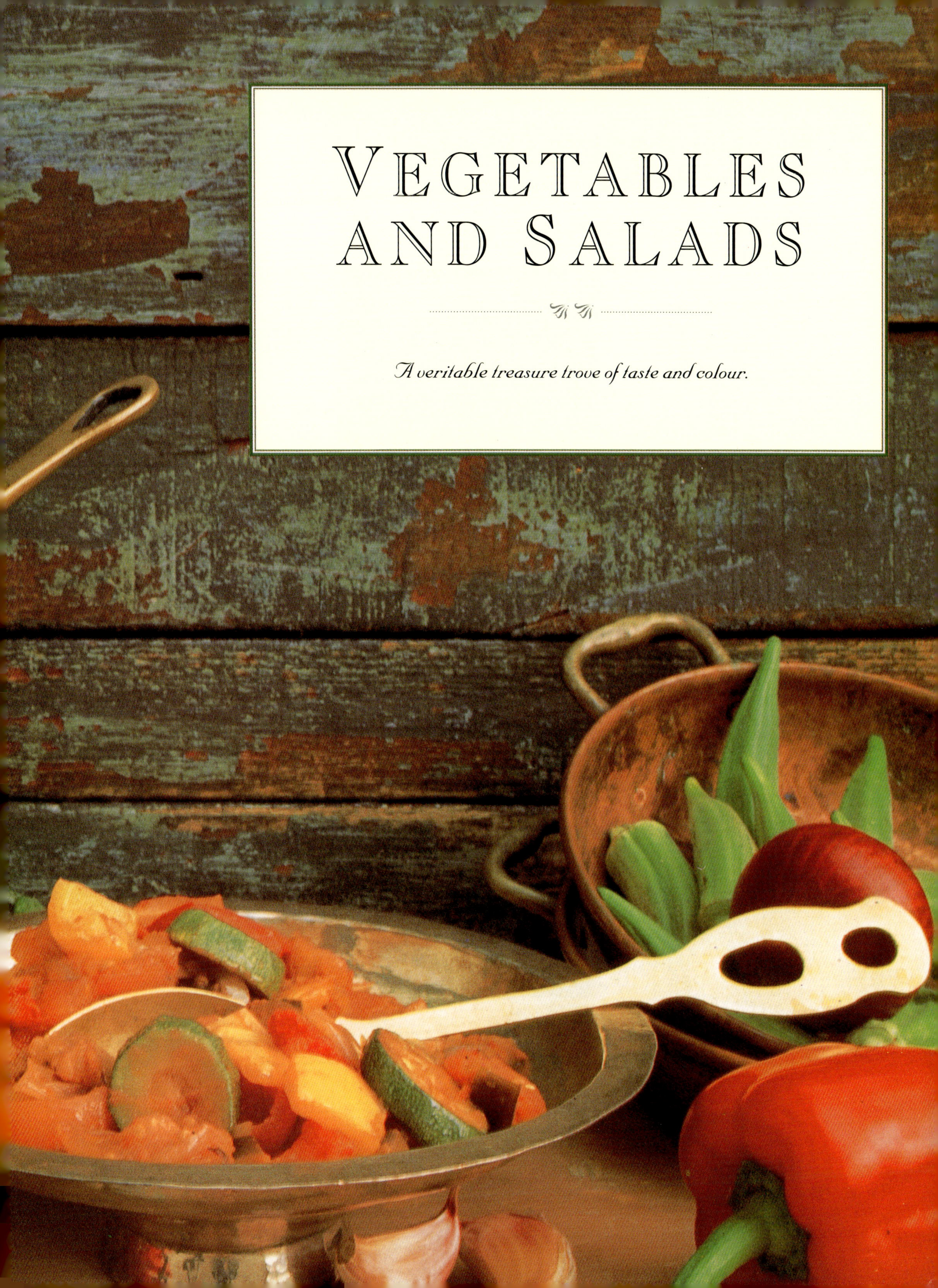

MARINATED MUSHROOMS

This Spanish recipe makes a nice change from the French classic, mushrooms à la Grecque. Make this dish the day before you eat it, the flavour will improve with keeping.

30ml/2 tbsp olive oil
1 small onion, very finely chopped
1 garlic clove, crushed
15ml/1 tbsp tomato purée
50ml/2fl oz/¼ cup dry white wine
2 cloves
pinch of saffron strands
225g/8oz button mushrooms, trimmed
salt and ground black pepper
chopped fresh parsley, to garnish

SERVES 4

1 Heat the oil in a pan. Add the onion and garlic and cook until soft. Stir in the tomato purée, wine, 50ml/2fl oz/¼ cup water, cloves and saffron and season with salt and pepper. Bring to the boil, cover and simmer gently for 45 minutes, adding more water if it becomes too dry.

2 Add the mushrooms to the pan, then cover and simmer for a further 5 minutes. Remove from the heat and, still covered, allow to cool. Chill in the fridge overnight. Serve cold, sprinkled with chopped parsley.

POTATO AND ONION TORTILLA

One of the signature dishes of Spain, this delicious thick potato and onion omelette is eaten at all times of the day, hot or cold.

300ml/½ pint/1¼ cups olive oil
6 large potatoes, peeled and sliced
2 Spanish onions, sliced
6 size 2 eggs
salt and ground black pepper
cherry tomatoes, halved, to serve

SERVES 4

1 Heat the oil in a large non-stick frying pan. Stir in the potato, onion and a little salt. Cover and cook gently for 20 minutes until soft.

2 Beat the eggs in a large bowl. Remove the onion and potato from the pan with a slotted spoon and add to the eggs. Season with salt and pepper to taste. Pour off some of the oil, leaving about 60ml/4 tbsp in the pan. (Reserve the leftover oil for other cooking.) Heat the pan again.

3 When the oil is very hot, pour in the egg mixture. Cook for 2–3 minutes. Cover the pan with a plate and invert the omelette on to it. Slide it back into the pan and cook for a further 5 minutes, until golden brown and moist in the middle. Serve in wedges, with the tomatoes.

SPANISH POTATOES

This is an adaptation of a peppery potato dish, of which there are several versions. All of them are fried and mildly spiced with the added tang of wine vinegar. Serve with cold meats or as a tapas.

675g/1½ lb small new potatoes
75ml/5 tbsp olive oil
2 garlic cloves, sliced
2.5ml/½ tsp crushed chillies
2.5ml/½ tsp ground cumin
10ml/2 tsp paprika
30ml/2 tbsp red or white wine vinegar
1 red or green pepper, seeded and sliced
coarse sea salt, to serve (optional)

SERVES 4

1 Cook the potatoes in boiling salted water until almost tender. Drain and, if preferred, peel them. Cut into chunks.

2 Heat the oil in a large frying or sauté pan and fry the potatoes, turning them frequently until golden.

3 Meanwhile, crush together the garlic, chillies and cumin using a pestle and mortar. Mix with the paprika and wine vinegar.

4 Add the garlic mixture to the potatoes with the sliced pepper and cook, stirring, for 2 minutes. Serve warm, or leave until cold. Scatter with coarse sea salt, if you like, to serve.

SWEET AND SOUR ONION SALAD

This recipe is primarily from Provence in the south of France but there are influences from other Mediterranean countries, too.

450g/1lb baby onions, peeled
50ml/2fl oz/¼ cup wine vinegar
45ml/3 tbsp olive oil
40g/1½oz/3 tbsp caster sugar
45ml/3 tbsp tomato purée
1 bay leaf
2 parsley sprigs
65g/2½oz/½ cup raisins
salt and ground black pepper

SERVES 6

1 Put all the ingredients in a pan with 300ml/½ pint/1¼ cups water. Bring to the boil and simmer gently, uncovered, for 45 minutes, or until the onions are tender and most of the liquid has evaporated.

2 Remove the bay leaf and parsley, check the seasoning, and transfer to a serving dish. Serve at room temperature.

TAPENADE AND HERB AÏOLI WITH SUMMER VEGETABLES

A beautiful platter of salad vegetables served with one or two interesting sauces makes a thoroughly appetizing and informal starter. This colourful French appetizer is perfect for entertaining as it can be prepared in advance.

FOR THE TAPENADE

175g/6oz/1½ cups pitted black olives
50g/2oz can anchovy fillets, drained
30ml/2 tbsp capers
120ml/4fl oz/½ cup olive oil
finely grated rind of 1 lemon
15ml/1 tbsp brandy (optional)
ground black pepper

FOR THE HERB AIOLI

2 egg yolks
5ml/1 tsp Dijon mustard
10ml/2 tsp white wine vinegar
250ml/8fl oz/1 cup light olive oil
45ml/3 tbsp chopped mixed fresh herbs, such as chervil, parsley or tarragon
30ml/2 tbsp chopped watercress
5 garlic cloves, crushed
salt and ground black pepper

TO SERVE

2 red peppers, seeded and cut into wide strips
30ml/2 tbsp olive oil
225g/8oz new potatoes
115g/4oz green beans
225g/8oz baby carrots
225g/8oz young asparagus
12 quail's eggs (optional)
fresh herbs, to garnish
coarse salt for sprinkling

SERVES 6

1 To make the tapenade, finely chop the olives, anchovies and capers and beat together with the oil, lemon rind and brandy if using. (Alternatively, lightly process the ingredients in a blender or food processor, scraping down the mixture from the sides of the bowl if necessary.)

2 Season with pepper and blend in a little more oil if the mixture is very dry. Transfer to a serving dish.

3 To make the aïoli, beat together the egg yolks, mustard and vinegar. Gradually blend in the oil, a trickle at a time, whisking well after each addition until thick and smooth. Season with salt and pepper to taste, adding a little more vinegar if the aïoli tastes bland.

4 Stir in the mixed herbs, watercress and garlic, then transfer to a serving dish. Cover and put in the fridge.

5 Put the peppers on a foil-lined grill rack and brush with the oil. Grill under a high heat until just beginning to char.

6 Cook the potatoes in a large pan of boiling, salted water until just tender. Add the beans and carrots and cook for 1 minute. Add the asparagus and cook for a further 30 seconds. Drain the vegetables.

7 Cook the quail's eggs in boiling water for 2 minutes. Drain and remove half of each shell.

8 Arrange all the vegetables, eggs and sauces on a serving platter. Garnish with fresh herbs and serve with coarse salt for sprinkling.

COOK'S TIP

Keep any leftover sauces for serving with salads. The tapenade is also delicious tossed with pasta or spread on to warm toast.

RATATOUILLE

A highly versatile vegetable stew from Provence. Ratatouille is delicious hot or cold, on its own or with eggs, pasta, fish or meat – particularly roast lamb.

900g/2lb ripe, well-flavoured tomatoes
120ml/4fl oz/½ cup olive oil
2 onions, thinly sliced
2 red peppers, seeded and cut into chunks
1 yellow or orange pepper, seeded and cut into chunks
1 large aubergine, cut into chunks
2 courgettes, cut into thick slices
4 garlic cloves, crushed
2 bay leaves
15ml/1 tbsp chopped young thyme
salt and ground black pepper

SERVES 6

1 Plunge the tomatoes into boiling water for 30 seconds, then refresh in cold water. Peel away the skins and chop roughly.

2 Heat a little of the oil in a large, heavy-based pan and fry the onions for 5 minutes. Add the peppers and fry for a further 2 minutes. Drain. Add the aubergines and more oil and fry gently for 5 minutes. Add the remaining oil and courgettes and fry for 3 minutes. Drain.

3 Add the garlic and tomatoes to the pan with the bay leaves and thyme and a little salt and pepper. Cook gently until the tomatoes have softened and are turning pulpy.

4 Return all the vegetables to the pan and cook gently, stirring frequently, for about 15 minutes, until fairly pulpy but retaining a little texture. Season with more salt and pepper to taste.

COOK'S TIP

There are no specific quantities for the vegetables when making ratatouille so you can, to a large extent, vary the quantities and types of vegetables depending on what you have in the fridge. If the tomatoes are a little tasteless, add 30–45ml/2–3 tbsp tomato purée and a dash of sugar to the mixture along with the tomatoes.

SPINACH WITH RAISINS AND PINE NUTS

Raisins and pine nuts are frequent partners in Spanish recipes. Here, tossed with wilted spinach and croûtons, they make a delicious snack or main meal accompaniment.

50g/2oz/⅓ cup raisins
1 thick slice crusty white bread
45ml/3 tbsp olive oil
25g/1oz/⅓ cup pine nuts
500g/1¼lb young spinach, stalks removed
2 garlic cloves, crushed
salt and ground black pepper

SERVES 4

1 Put the raisins in a small bowl with boiling water and leave to soak for 10 minutes. Drain.

2 Cut the bread into cubes and discard the crusts. Heat 30ml/2 tbsp of the oil and fry the bread until golden. Drain.

3 Heat the remaining oil in the pan. Fry the pine nuts until beginning to colour. Add the spinach and garlic and cook quickly, turning the spinach until it has just wilted.

4 Toss in the raisins and season lightly with salt and pepper. Transfer to a warmed serving dish. Scatter with croûtons and serve hot.

VARIATION

Use Swiss chard or spinach beet instead of the spinach, cooking them a little longer.

STUFFED TOMATOES AND PEPPERS

Colourful peppers and tomatoes make perfect containers for various meat and vegetable stuffings. This rice and herb version uses typically Greek ingredients.

VARIATION

Small aubergines or large courgettes also make good vegetables for stuffing. Halve and scoop out the centres of the vegetables, then oil the vegetable cases and bake for about 15 minutes. Chop the centres, fry for 2–3 minutes to soften and add to the stuffing mixture. Fill the aubergine or courgette cases with the stuffing and bake as for the peppers and tomatoes.

2 large ripe tomatoes
1 green pepper
1 yellow or orange pepper
60ml/4 tbsp olive oil, plus extra for sprinkling
2 onions, chopped
2 garlic cloves, crushed
50g/2oz/½ cup blanched almonds, chopped
75g/3oz/scant ½ cup long grain rice, boiled and drained
15g/½oz mint, roughly chopped
15g/½oz parsley, roughly chopped
25g/1oz/2 tbsp sultanas
45ml/3 tbsp ground almonds
salt and ground black pepper
chopped mixed herbs, to garnish

SERVES 4

1 Preheat the oven to 190°C/375°F/Gas 5. Cut the tomatoes in half and scoop out the pulp and seeds using a teaspoon. Leave the tomatoes to drain on kitchen paper with cut sides down. Roughly chop the tomato pulp and seeds.

2 Halve the peppers, leaving the cores intact. Scoop out the seeds. Brush the peppers with 15ml/1 tbsp of the oil and bake on a baking tray for 15 minutes. Place the peppers and tomatoes in a shallow ovenproof dish and season with salt and pepper.

3 Fry the onions in the remaining oil for 5 minutes. Add the garlic and chopped almonds and fry for a further minute.

4 Remove the pan from the heat and stir in the rice, chopped tomatoes, mint, parsley and sultanas. Season well with salt and pepper and spoon the mixture into the tomatoes and peppers.

5 Pour 150ml/¼ pint/⅔ cup boiling water around the tomatoes and peppers and bake, uncovered, for 20 minutes. Scatter with the ground almonds and sprinkle with a little extra olive oil. Return to the oven and bake for a further 20 minutes, or until turning golden. Serve garnished with fresh herbs.

FISH AND SEAFOOD

Mediterranean fishermen reap a rich harvest of fish and seafood, which are often simply grilled or fried, or used as the basis of a soup or stew.

SEAFOOD RISOTTO

Risotto is one of Italy's most popular rice dishes and it is made with everything from pumpkin to squid ink. On the Mediterranean shores, seafood is the most obvious addition.

60ml/4 tbsp sunflower oil
1 onion, chopped
2 garlic cloves, crushed
225g/8oz/generous 1 cup arborio rice
105ml/7 tbsp white wine
1.5 litres/2½ pints/6¼ cups hot fish stock
350g/12oz mixed seafood, such as raw prawns, mussels, squid rings or clams
grated rind of ½ lemon
30ml/2 tbsp tomato purée
15ml/1 tbsp chopped fresh parsley
salt and ground black pepper

SERVES 4

1 Heat the oil in a heavy-based pan, add the onion and garlic and cook until soft. Add the rice and stir to coat the grains with oil. Add the wine and cook over a moderate heat, stirring, for a few minutes until absorbed.

2 Add 150ml/¼ pint/⅔ cup of the hot stock and cook, stirring constantly, until the liquid is absorbed by the rice. Continue stirring and adding stock in 150ml/¼ pint/⅔ cup quantities, until half is left. This should take about 10 minutes.

3 Stir in the seafood and cook for 2–3 minutes. Add the remaining stock as before, until the rice is cooked. It should be quite creamy and the grains *al dente*.

4 Stir in the lemon rind, tomato purée and parsley. Season with salt and pepper and serve warm.

ITALIAN PRAWN SKEWERS

Simple and delicious mouthfuls from the Amalfi Coast.

900g/2lb raw tiger prawns, peeled
60ml/4 tbsp olive oil
45ml/3 tbsp vegetable oil
75g/3oz/1¼ cups very fine dry breadcrumbs
1 garlic clove, crushed
15ml/1 tbsp chopped fresh parsley
salt and ground black pepper
lemon wedges, to serve

SERVES 4

1 Slit the prawns down their backs and remove the dark vein. Rinse in cold water and pat dry.

2 Put the olive oil and vegetable oil in a large bowl and add the prawns, mixing them to coat evenly. Add the breadcrumbs, garlic and parsley and season with salt and pepper. Toss the prawns thoroughly, to give them an even coating of breadcrumbs. Cover and leave to marinate for 1 hour.

3 Thread the prawns on to four metal or wooden skewers, curling them up as you do so, so that the tail is skewered in the middle.

4 Preheat the grill. Place the skewers in the grill pan and cook for about 2 minutes on each side, until the breadcrumbs are golden. Serve with lemon wedges.

Hake and Clams with Salsa Verde

Hake is one of the most popular fish in Spain and here it is cooked in a sauce flavoured with parsley, lemon juice and garlic.

4 hake steaks, about 2cm/¾in thick
50g/2oz/½ cup plain flour for dusting, plus 30ml/2 tbsp
60ml/4 tbsp olive oil
15ml/1 tbsp lemon juice
1 small onion, finely chopped
4 garlic cloves, crushed
150ml/¼ pint/⅔ cup fish stock
150ml/¼ pint/⅔ cup white wine
90ml/6 tbsp chopped fresh parsley
75g/3oz frozen petits pois
16 fresh clams
salt and ground black pepper

Serves 4

1 Preheat the oven to 180°C/350°F/Gas 4. Season the fish with salt and pepper, then dust both sides with flour. Heat 30ml/2 tbsp of the oil in a large sauté pan, add the fish and fry for about 1 minute on each side. Transfer to an ovenproof dish and sprinkle with lemon juice.

2 Clean the pan, then heat the remaining oil. Add the onion and garlic and cook until soft. Stir in 30ml/2 tbsp flour and cook for about 1 minute. Gradually add the stock and wine, stirring until thickened and smooth. Add 75ml/5 tbsp of the parsley and the petits pois and season with salt and pepper.

3 Pour the sauce over the fish, and bake in the oven for 15–20 minutes, adding the clams to the dish 3–4 minutes before the end of the cooking time. Discard any clams that do not open, then sprinkle with the remaining parsley before serving.

COD PLAKI

Greece has so much coastline, it's no wonder that fish is popular all over the country. Generally, it is treated very simply, but this recipe is a little more involved, baking the fish with onions and tomatoes.

300ml/½ pint/1¼ cups olive oil
2 onions, thinly sliced
3 large well-flavoured tomatoes, roughly chopped
3 garlic cloves, thinly sliced
5ml/1 tsp sugar
5ml/1 tsp chopped fresh dill
5ml/1 tsp chopped fresh mint
5ml/1 tsp chopped fresh celery leaves
15ml/1 tbsp chopped fresh parsley
6 cod steaks
juice of 1 lemon
salt and ground black pepper
extra dill, mint or parsley, to garnish

SERVES 6

1 Heat the oil in a large sauté pan or flameproof dish. Add the onions and cook until pale golden. Add the tomatoes, garlic, sugar, dill, mint, celery leaves and parsley with 300ml/½ pint/1¼ cups water. Season with salt and pepper, then simmer, uncovered, for 25 minutes, until the liquid has reduced by one-third.

2 Add the fish steaks and cook gently for 10–12 minutes, until the fish is just cooked. Remove from the heat and add the lemon juice (*left*). Cover and leave to stand for about 20 minutes before serving. Arrange the cod in a dish and spoon the sauce over. Garnish with herbs and serve warm or cold.

MOUCLADE OF MUSSELS

This recipe is quite similar to Moules Marinière but has the additional flavouring of fennel and mild curry. Traditionally the mussels are shelled and piled into scallop shells, but nothing beats a bowlful of steaming hot, garlicky mussels, served in their own glistening shells.

1.75kg/4½lb fresh mussels
250ml/8fl oz/1 cup dry white wine
good pinch of grated nutmeg
3 thyme sprigs
2 bay leaves
1 small onion, finely chopped
50g/2oz/¼ cup butter
1 fennel bulb, thinly sliced
4 garlic cloves, crushed
2.5ml/½ tsp curry paste or powder
30ml/2 tbsp plain flour
150ml/¼ pint/⅔ cup double cream
ground black pepper
chopped fresh dill, to garnish

SERVES 6

1 Scrub the mussels, discarding any that are damaged or open ones that do not close when tapped with a knife.

2 Put the wine, nutmeg, thyme, bay leaves and onion in a large saucepan and bring just to the boil. Tip in the mussels and cover with a lid. Cook for 4–5 minutes until the mussels have opened.

3 Drain the mussels, reserving all the juices. Discard any mussels that remain closed.

4 Melt the butter in a large clean pan and gently fry the fennel slices and garlic for about 5 minutes until softened.

5 Stir in the curry paste or powder and flour and cook for 1 minute. Remove from the heat and gradually blend in the cooking juices from the mussels. Return to the heat and cook, stirring, for 2 minutes.

6 Stir in the cream and a little pepper. Add the mussels to the pan and heat through for 2 minutes. Serve hot, garnished with dill.

VARIATION

Saffron is a popular addition to a mouclade. Soak 2.5ml/½ tsp saffron strands in a little boiling water and add to the sauce with the stock.

BRODETTO

The different regions of Italy have their own variations of this dish, but all require a good fish stock. Make sure you buy some of the fish whole so you can simply simmer them, remove the cooked flesh and strain the deliciously flavoured juices to make the stock.

900g/2lb mixture of fish fillets or steaks, such as monkfish, cod, haddock, halibut or hake
900g/2lb mixture of conger eel, red or grey mullet, snapper or small white fish
1 onion, halved
1 celery stick, roughly chopped
225g/8oz squid
225g/8oz fresh mussels
675g/1½lb ripe tomatoes
60ml/4 tbsp olive oil
1 large onion, thinly sliced
3 garlic cloves, crushed
5ml/1 tsp saffron strands
150ml/¼ pint/⅔ cup dry white wine
90ml/6 tbsp chopped fresh parsley
salt and ground black pepper
croûtons, to serve

SERVES 4–5

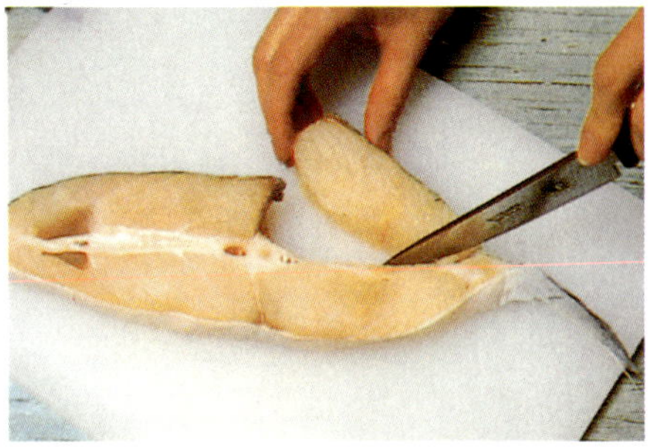

1. Remove any skin and bones from the fish fillets or steaks, cut the fish into large pieces and reserve. Place the bones in a pan with all the remaining fish.

2. Add the halved onion and the celery and just cover with water. Bring almost to the boil, then reduce the heat and simmer gently for about 30 minutes. Lift out the fish and remove the flesh from the bones. Reserve the stock.

3. To prepare the squid, twist the head and tentacles away from the body. Cut the head from the tentacles. Discard the body contents and peel away the mottled skin. Wash the tentacles and bodies and dry on kitchen paper.

COOK'S TIP

To make the croûtons, cut thin slices from a long thin stick of bread and shallow fry in a little butter until golden.

4. Scrub the mussels, discarding any that are damaged or open ones that do not close when tapped.

5. Plunge the tomatoes into boiling water for 30 seconds, then refresh in cold water. Peel away the skins and chop roughly.

6. Heat the oil in a large saucepan or sauté pan. Add the sliced onion and the garlic and fry gently for 3 minutes. Add the squid and the uncooked white fish, which you reserved earlier, and fry quickly on all sides. Drain.

7. Add 475ml/16fl oz/2 cups strained reserved fish stock, the saffron and tomatoes to the pan. Pour in the wine. Bring to the boil, then reduce the heat and simmer for about 5 minutes. Add the mussels, cover, and cook for 3–4 minutes until the mussels have opened. Discard any that remain closed.

8. Season the sauce with salt and pepper and put all the fish in the pan. Cook gently for 5 minutes. Scatter with the parsley and serve with the croûtons.

SARDINE GRATIN

In Sicily and other countries in the Western Mediterranean, sardines are filled with a robust stuffing, flavoursome enough to compete with the rich oiliness of the fish itself.

15ml/1 tbsp light olive oil
½ small onion, finely chopped
2 garlic cloves, crushed
40g/1½oz/6 tbsp blanched almonds, chopped
25g/1oz/2 tbsp sultanas, roughly chopped
10 pitted black olives
30ml/2 tbsp capers, roughly chopped
30ml/2 tbsp roughly chopped fresh parsley
50g/2oz/1 cup breadcrumbs
16 large sardines, scaled and gutted
25g/1oz/⅓ cup grated Parmesan cheese
salt and ground black pepper
flat leaf parsley, to garnish

SERVES 4

1 Preheat the oven to 200°C/400°F/Gas 6. Lightly oil a large shallow ovenproof dish.

2 Heat the oil in a frying pan and fry the onion and garlic gently for 3 minutes. Stir in the almonds, sultanas, olives, capers, parsley and 25g/1oz/¼ cup of the breadcrumbs. Season lightly with salt and pepper.

ABOVE: Brodetto (top) and Sardine Gratin (bottom).

3 Make 2–3 diagonal cuts on each side of the sardines. Pack the stuffing into the cavities and lay the sardines in the prepared dish.

4 Mix the remaining breadcrumbs with the cheese and scatter over the fish. Bake for about 20 minutes until the fish is cooked through. Test by piercing one sardine through the thickest part with a knife. Garnish with parsley and serve immediately with a leafy salad.

ZARZUELA

Zarzuela means "light opera" or "musical comedy" in Spanish and the classic fish stew of the same name should be as lively and colourful as the zarzuela itself. This feast of fish includes lobster and other shellfish, but you can modify the ingredients to suit the occasion and availability.

1 cooked lobster
24 fresh mussels or clams
1 large monkfish tail
225g/8oz squid rings
15ml/1 tbsp plain flour
90ml/6 tbsp olive oil
12 large raw prawns
450g/1lb ripe tomatoes
2 large mild onions, chopped
4 garlic cloves, crushed
30ml/2 tbsp brandy
2 bay leaves
5ml/1 tsp paprika
1 red chilli, seeded and chopped
300ml/½ pint/1¼ cups fish stock
15g/½oz/2 tbsp ground almonds
30ml/2 tbsp chopped fresh parsley
salt and ground black pepper

SERVES 6

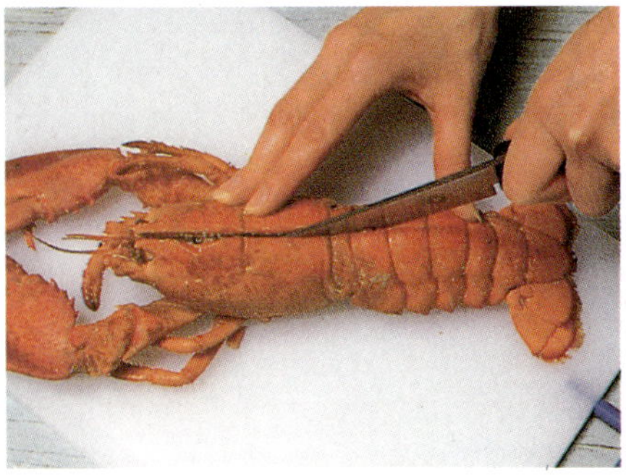

1 Using a large knife, cut the lobster in half lengthways. Remove the dark intestine that runs down the length of the tail. Crack the claws using a hammer.

2 Scrub the mussels, discarding any that are damaged or open ones that do not close when tapped with a knife. Cut the monkfish fillets away from the central cartilage and cut each fillet into three.

3 Toss the monkfish and squid in seasoned flour. Heat the oil in a large frying pan. Add the monkfish and squid and fry quickly; remove from the pan. Fry the prawns on both sides, then remove from the pan.

4 Plunge the tomatoes into boiling water for 30 seconds, then refresh in cold water. Peel away the skins and chop roughly.

5 Add the onions and two-thirds of the garlic to the frying pan and fry for 3 minutes. Add the brandy and ignite with a taper. When the flames die down, add the tomatoes, bay leaves, paprika, chilli and stock.

6 Bring to the boil, reduce the heat and simmer gently for 5 minutes. Add the mussels or clams, cover and cook for 3–4 minutes, until the shells have opened.

7 Remove the mussels or clams from the sauce and discard any that remain closed.

8 Arrange all the fish, including the lobster, in a large flameproof serving dish. Blend the ground almonds to a paste with the remaining garlic and parsley and stir into the sauce. Season with salt and pepper.

9 Pour the sauce over the fish and lobster and cook gently for about 5 minutes until hot. Serve immediately with a green salad and plenty of warmed bread.

MEAT, POULTRY AND GAME

At the heart of all Mediterranean cuisines.

ROAST LOIN OF PORK STUFFED WITH FIGS, OLIVES AND ALMONDS

Pork is a popular meat in Spain, and this recipe using fruit and nuts in the stuffing is of Catalan influence, where the combination of meat and fruit is quite common.

60ml/4 tbsp olive oil
1 onion, finely chopped
2 garlic cloves, chopped
75g/3oz/1½ cups fresh breadcrumbs
4 ready-to-eat dried figs, chopped
8 pitted green olives, chopped
25g/1oz/¼ cup flaked almonds
15ml/1 tbsp lemon juice
15ml/1 tbsp chopped fresh parsley
1 egg yolk
900g/2lb boned loin of pork
salt and ground black pepper

SERVES 4

1 Preheat the oven to 200°C/400°F/Gas 6. Heat 45ml/3 tbsp of the oil in a pan, add the onion and garlic, and cook gently until softened. Remove the pan from the heat and stir in the breadcrumbs, figs, olives, almonds, lemon juice, parsley and egg yolk. Season to taste.

COOK'S TIP

Keep a tub of breadcrumbs in the freezer. They can be used frozen.

2 Remove any string from the pork and unroll the belly flap, cutting away any excess fat or meat, to enable you to do so. Spread half the stuffing over the flat piece and roll up, starting from the thick side. Tie at intervals with string.

3 Pour the remaining oil into a small roasting tin and put in the pork. Roast for 1 hour 15 minutes. Form the remaining stuffing mixture into balls and add to the roasting tin around the meat, 15–20 minutes before the end of cooking time.

4 Remove the pork from the oven and let it rest for 10 minutes. Carve into thick slices and serve with the stuffing balls and any juices from the tin. This is also good served cold.

Spanish Pork and Sausage Casserole

Another pork dish from the Catalan region of Spain, which uses the spicy butifarra sausage. You can find these sausages in some Spanish delicatessens but, if not, sweet Italian sausages will do.

30ml/2 tbsp olive oil
4 boneless pork chops, about 175g/6oz
4 butifarra or sweet Italian sausages
1 onion, chopped
2 garlic cloves, chopped
120ml/4fl oz/½ cup dry white wine
4 plum tomatoes, chopped
1 bay leaf
30ml/2 tbsp chopped fresh parsley
salt and ground black pepper
green salad and baked potatoes, to serve

Serves 4

1 Heat the oil in a large deep frying pan. Cook the pork chops over a high heat until browned on both sides, then transfer to a plate.

2 Add the sausages, onion and garlic to the pan and cook over a moderate heat until the sausages are browned and the onion softened, turning the sausages two or three times during cooking. Return the chops to the pan.

3 Stir in the wine, tomatoes and bay leaf, and season with salt and pepper. Add the parsley. Cover the pan and cook for 30 minutes.

4 Remove the sausages from the pan and cut into thick slices. Return them to the pan and heat through. Serve hot, accompanied by a green salad and baked potatoes.

Cook's Tip

Vine tomatoes, which are making a welcome appearance in our supermarkets, can be used instead of plum tomatoes.

CORSICAN BEEF STEW WITH MACARONI

Pasta is eaten in many parts of the Mediterranean. In Corsica, it's often served with gravy as a sauce and, in this case, a rich beef stew.

25g/1oz dried mushrooms (ceps or porcini)
6 garlic cloves
900g/2lb stewing beef, cut into 5cm/2in cubes
115g/4oz lardons, or thick streaky bacon cut into strips
45ml/3 tbsp olive oil
2 onions, sliced
300ml/½ pint/1¼ cups dry white wine
30ml/2 tbsp passata
pinch of ground cinnamon
sprig of rosemary
1 bay leaf
225g/8oz/2 cups large macaroni
50g/2oz/⅔ cup freshly grated Parmesan cheese
salt and ground black pepper

SERVES 4

1 Soak the dried mushrooms in warm water for 30 minutes. Drain, set the mushrooms aside and reserve the liquid. Cut three of the garlic cloves into thin strips and insert into the pieces of beef by making little slits with a sharp knife. Push the lardons or pieces of bacon into the beef with the garlic. Season the meat with salt and pepper.

2 Heat the oil in a heavy-based pan, add half the beef and brown well on all sides. Repeat with the remaining beef. Transfer to a plate. Add the sliced onions to the pan and cook until lightly browned. Crush the remaining garlic and add to the onions with the meat.

3 Stir in the white wine, passata, mushrooms, cinnamon, rosemary and bay leaf and season with salt and pepper. Cook gently for 30 minutes, stirring often. Strain the mushroom liquid and add to the stew with enough water to cover. Bring to the boil, cover and simmer very gently for 3 hours, until the meat is very tender.

4 Cook the macaroni in a large pan of boiling, salted water for 10 minutes, or until *al dente*. Lift the pieces of meat out of the gravy and transfer to a warmed serving platter. Drain the pasta and layer in a serving bowl with the gravy and cheese. Serve with the meat.

PROVENÇAL BEEF AND OLIVE DAUBE

A daube is a French method of braising meat with wine and herbs. This version from the Nice area in the south of France also includes black olives and tomatoes.

1.5kg/3–3½lb topside beef
225g/8oz lardons, or thick streaky bacon cut into strips
225g/8oz carrots, sliced
1 bay leaf
1 thyme sprig
2 parsley stalks
3 garlic cloves
225g/8oz/2 cups pitted black olives
400g/14oz can chopped tomatoes
crusty bread, flageolet beans or pasta, to serve

FOR THE MARINADE

120ml/4fl oz/½ cup extra virgin olive oil
1 onion, sliced
4 shallots, sliced
1 celery stick, sliced
1 carrot, sliced
150ml/¼ pint/⅔ cup red wine
6 peppercorns
2 garlic cloves, sliced
1 bay leaf
1 thyme sprig
2 parsley stalks
salt

SERVES 6

1 To make the marinade, heat the oil in a large shallow pan, add the onion, shallots, celery and carrot. Cook for 2 minutes, then lower the heat and add the red wine, peppercorns, garlic, bay leaf, thyme and parsley stalks. Season with salt, then cover and leave to simmer gently for 15–20 minutes. Set aside.

2 Place the beef in a large glass or earthenware dish and pour over the cooled marinade. Cover the dish and leave to marinate in a cool place or in the fridge for 12 hours, turning the meat once or twice.

3 Preheat the oven to 160°C/325°F/Gas 3. Lift the meat out of the marinade and fit snugly into an ovenproof casserole. Add the lardons or bacon and carrots, along with the herbs and garlic. Strain in all the marinade. Cover the casserole with greaseproof paper, then the lid and cook in the oven for 2½ hours.

4 Remove the casserole from the oven and stir in the olives and tomatoes. Re-cover the casserole, return to the oven and cook for a further 30 minutes. Serve the meat cut into thick slices, accompanied by crusty bread, beans or pasta.

LAMB CASSEROLE WITH GARLIC AND BROAD BEANS

This recipe has a Spanish influence and makes a substantial meal, served with potatoes. It's based on stewing lamb with a large amount of garlic and sherry – the addition of broad beans gives colour.

45ml/3 tbsp olive oil
1.5kg/3–3½lb fillet lamb, cut into 5cm/2in cubes
1 large onion, chopped
6 large garlic cloves, unpeeled
1 bay leaf
5ml/1 tsp paprika
120ml/4fl oz/½ cup dry sherry
115g/4oz shelled fresh or frozen broad beans
30ml/2 tbsp chopped fresh parsley
salt and ground black pepper

SERVES 6

1 Heat 30ml/2 tbsp of the oil in a large flameproof casserole. Add half the meat and brown well on all sides. Transfer to a plate. Brown the rest of the meat in the same way and remove from the casserole.

2 Heat the remaining oil in the pan, add the onion and cook for about 5 minutes until soft. Return the meat to the casserole.

3 Add the garlic cloves, bay leaf, paprika and sherry. Season with salt and pepper. Bring to the boil, then cover and simmer very gently for 1½–2 hours, until the meat is tender.

4 Add the broad beans about 10 minutes before the end of the cooking time. Stir in the parsley just before serving.

CHICKEN WITH CHORIZO

The addition of chorizo sausage and sherry gives a warm, interesting flavour to this simple Spanish casserole. Serve with rice or boiled potatoes.

1 medium chicken, jointed, or
4 chicken legs, halved
10ml/2 tsp ground paprika
60ml/4 tbsp olive oil
2 small onions, sliced
6 garlic cloves, thinly sliced
150g/5oz chorizo sausage
400g/14oz can chopped tomatoes
12–16 bay leaves
75ml/5 tbsp medium sherry
salt and ground black pepper
rice or potatoes, to serve

SERVES 4

1 Preheat the oven to 190°C/375°F/Gas 5. Coat the chicken pieces in the paprika, making sure they are evenly covered, then season with salt. Heat the olive oil in a frying pan and fry the chicken until brown.

2 Transfer to an ovenproof dish. Add the onions to the pan and fry quickly. Add the garlic and sliced chorizo and fry for 2 minutes.

3 Add the tomatoes, two of the bay leaves and sherry and bring to the boil. Pour over the chicken and cover with a lid. Bake for 45 minutes. Remove the lid and season to taste. Cook for a further 20 minutes until the chicken is tender and golden. Serve with rice or potatoes, garnished with bay leaves.

CHICKEN CASSEROLE WITH SPICED FIGS

The Spanish Catalans have various recipes for fruit with meat. This is quite an unusual one, but it uses one of the fruits most strongly associated with the Mediterranean – the fig.

FOR THE FIGS

150g/5oz/⅔ cup granulated sugar
120ml/4fl oz/½ cup white wine vinegar
1 lemon slice
1 cinnamon stick
450g/1lb fresh figs

FOR THE CHICKEN

120ml/4fl oz/½ cup medium sweet white wine
pared rind of ½ lemon
1.5kg/3–3½lb chicken, jointed into eight pieces
50g/2oz lardons, or thick streaky bacon cut into strips
15ml/1 tbsp olive oil
50ml/2fl oz/¼ cup chicken stock
salt and ground black pepper

SERVES 4

1 Put the sugar, vinegar, lemon slice and cinnamon stick in a pan with 120ml/4fl oz/½ cup water. Bring to the boil, then simmer for 5 minutes. Add the figs, cover, and simmer for 10 minutes. Remove from heat, cover, and leave for 3 hours.

2 Preheat the oven to 180°C/350°F/Gas 4. Drain the figs, and place in a bowl. Add the wine and lemon rind. Season the chicken. In a large frying pan cook the lardons or streaky bacon strips until the fat melts and they turn golden. Transfer to a shallow ovenproof dish, leaving any fat in the pan. Add the oil to the pan and brown the chicken pieces all over.

3 Drain the figs, adding the wine to the pan with the chicken. Boil until the sauce has reduced and is syrupy. Transfer the contents of the frying pan to the ovenproof dish and cook in the oven, uncovered, for about 20 minutes. Add the figs and chicken stock, cover and return to the oven for a further 10 minutes. Serve with a green salad.

Chicken and Apricot Filo Pie

The filling for this pie has a Middle Eastern flavour – minced chicken combined with apricots, bulgur wheat, nuts and spices.

75g/3oz/½ cup bulgur wheat
75g/3oz/6 tbsp butter
1 onion, chopped
450g/1lb minced chicken
50g/2oz/¼ cup ready-to-eat dried apricots, finely chopped
25g/1oz/¼ cup blanched almonds, chopped
5ml/1 tsp ground cinnamon
2.5ml/½ tsp ground allspice
50ml/2fl oz/¼ cup Greek yogurt
15ml/1 tbsp snipped fresh chives
30ml/2 tbsp chopped fresh parsley
6 large sheets filo pastry
salt and ground black pepper
chives, to garnish

Serves 6

1 Preheat the oven to 200°C/400°F/Gas 6. Put the bulgur wheat in a bowl with 120ml/4fl oz/½ cup boiling water. Soak for 5–10 minutes, until the water is absorbed.

2 Heat 25g/1oz/2 tbsp of the butter in a pan, and gently fry the onion and chicken until pale golden.

3 Stir in the apricots, almonds and bulgur wheat and cook for a further 2 minutes. Remove from the heat and stir in the cinnamon, allspice, yogurt, chives and parsley. Season to taste with salt and pepper.

4 Melt the remaining butter. Unroll the filo pastry and cut into 25cm/10in rounds. Keep the pastry rounds covered with a clean, damp dish towel to prevent drying.

5 Line a 23cm/9in loose-based flan tin with three of the pastry rounds, brushing each one with butter as you layer them. Spoon in the chicken mixture, cover with three more pastry rounds, brushed with melted butter as before.

6 Crumple the remaining rounds and place them on top of the pie, then brush over any remaining melted butter. Bake the pie for about 30 minutes, until the pastry is golden brown and crisp. Serve Chicken and Apricot Filo Pie hot or cold, cut in wedges and garnished with chives.

Circassian Chicken

This is a Turkish dish, which is popular all over the Middle East. The chicken is poached and served cold with a flavoursome walnut sauce.

1.5kg/3–3½ lb chicken
2 onions, quartered
1 carrot, sliced
1 celery stick, trimmed and sliced
6 peppercorns
3 slices bread, crusts removed
2 garlic cloves, roughly chopped
400g/14oz/3½ cups chopped walnuts
15ml/1 tbsp walnut oil
salt and ground black pepper
chopped walnuts and paprika, to garnish

SERVES 6

1 Place the chicken in a large pan, with the onions, carrot, celery and peppercorns. Add enough water to cover, and bring to the boil. Simmer for about 1 hour, uncovered, until the chicken is tender. Leave to cool in the stock. Drain the chicken, reserving the stock.

2 Tear up the bread and soak in 90ml/6 tbsp of the chicken stock. Transfer to a blender or food processor, with the garlic and walnuts, and add 250ml/8fl oz/1 cup of the remaining stock. Process until smooth, then transfer to a pan.

3 Over a low heat, gradually add more chicken stock to the sauce, stirring constantly, until it is of a thick pouring consistency. Season with salt and pepper, remove from the heat and leave to cool in the pan. Skin and bone the chicken, and cut into bite-size chunks.

4 Place in a bowl and add a little of the sauce. Stir to coat the chicken, then arrange on a serving dish. Spoon the remaining sauce over the chicken, and drizzle with the walnut oil. Sprinkle with walnuts and paprika and serve at once.

CHICKEN WITH LEMONS AND OLIVES

Preserved lemons and limes are frequently used in Mediterranean cookery, particularly in North Africa where their gentle flavour enhances all kinds of meat and fish dishes.

2.5ml/½ tsp ground cinnamon
2.5ml/½ tsp ground turmeric
1.5kg/3–3½lb chicken
30ml/2 tbsp olive oil
1 large onion, thinly sliced
5cm/2in piece fresh root ginger, grated
600ml/1 pint/2½ cups chicken stock
2 preserved lemons or limes, or fresh, cut into wedges
75g/3oz/½ cup pitted brown olives
15ml/1 tbsp clear honey
60ml/4 tbsp chopped fresh coriander
salt and ground black pepper
coriander sprigs, to garnish

SERVES 4

1. Preheat the oven to 190°C/375°F/Gas 5. Mix the ground cinnamon and turmeric in a bowl with a little salt and pepper and rub all over the chicken skin to give an even coating.

2. Heat the oil in a large sauté or shallow frying pan and fry the chicken on all sides until it turns golden. Transfer the chicken to an ovenproof dish.

3. Add the sliced onion to the pan and fry for 3 minutes. Stir in the grated ginger and the chicken stock and bring just to the boil. Pour over the chicken, cover with a lid and bake in the oven for 30 minutes.

4. Remove the chicken from the oven and add the lemons or limes, brown olives and honey. Bake, uncovered, for a further 45 minutes until the chicken is tender.

5. Stir in the coriander and season to taste. Garnish with coriander sprigs and serve at once.

CASSOULET

Cassoulet is a classic French dish in which a feast of various meats is baked slowly with beans under a golden crumb crust. It is hearty and rich, perfect for a winter gathering.

675g/1½lb/3½ cups dried haricot beans
900g/2lb salt belly pork
4 large duck breasts
60ml/4 tbsp olive oil
2 onions, chopped
6 garlic cloves, crushed
2 bay leaves
1.5ml/¼ tsp ground cloves
60ml/4 tbsp tomato purée
8 good-quality sausages
4 tomatoes
75g/3oz/1½ cups stale breadcrumbs
salt and ground black pepper

SERVES 6–8

1 Put the beans in a large bowl and cover with plenty of cold water. Leave to soak overnight. If using salted belly pork, soak it overnight in water.

2 Drain the beans thoroughly and put them in a large saucepan with fresh water to cover. Bring to the boil and boil rapidly for 10 minutes. Drain and set the beans aside.

3 Cut the pork into large pieces, discarding the rind. Halve the duck breasts.

4 Heat 30ml/2 tbsp of the oil in a frying pan and fry the pork in batches, until browned.

5 Put the beans in a large, heavy-based saucepan with the onions, garlic, bay leaves, ground cloves and tomato purée. Stir in the browned pork and just cover with water. Bring to the boil, then reduce the heat to the lowest setting and simmer, covered, for about 1½ hours until the beans are tender.

6 Preheat the oven to 180°C/350°F/Gas 4. Heat the rest of the oil in a frying pan and fry the duck breasts and sausages until browned. Cut the sausages into smaller pieces.

7 Plunge the tomatoes into boiling water for 30 seconds, then refresh in cold water. Peel away the skins and cut them into quarters.

8 Transfer the bean mixture to a large earthenware pot or ovenproof dish and stir in the fried sausages and duck breasts and chopped tomatoes with salt and pepper to taste.

9 Sprinkle with an even layer of breadcrumbs and bake in the oven for 45 minutes to 1 hour until the crust is golden. Serve hot.

VARIATION

You can easily alter the proportions and types of meat and vegetables in a cassoulet. Turnips, carrots and celeriac make suitable vegetable substitutes while cubed lamb and goose can replace the pork and duck.

RABBIT SALMOREJO

Small pieces of jointed rabbit, conveniently sold in packs at the supermarket, make an interesting alternative to chicken in this light, spicy sauté from Spain. Serve with a simple dressed salad.

675g/1½lb rabbit portions
300ml/½ pint/1¼ cups dry white wine
15ml/1 tbsp sherry vinegar
several oregano sprigs
2 bay leaves
90ml/6 tbsp olive oil
175g/6oz baby onions, peeled and left whole
1 red chilli, seeded and finely chopped
4 garlic cloves, sliced
10ml/2 tsp paprika
150ml/¼ pint/⅔ cup chicken stock
salt and ground black pepper
flat leaf parsley sprigs, to garnish

SERVES 4

1 Put the rabbit in a bowl. Add the wine, vinegar, oregano and bay leaves and toss together lightly. Cover and leave to marinate for several hours or overnight.

2 Drain the rabbit, reserving the marinade, and pat dry on kitchen paper. Heat the oil in a large sauté or frying pan. Add the rabbit and fry on all sides until golden, then remove with a slotted spoon. Fry the onions until beginning to colour.

3 Remove the onions from the pan and add the chilli, garlic and paprika. Cook, stirring for about a minute. Add the reserved marinade, with the stock. Season lightly.

4 Return the rabbit to the pan with the onions. Bring to the boil, then reduce the heat and cover with a lid. Simmer very gently for about 45 minutes until the rabbit is tender. Serve garnished with a few sprigs of flat leaf parsley, if you like.

COOK'S TIP
If more convenient, rather than cooking on the hob, transfer the stew to an ovenproof dish and bake in the oven at 180°C/350°F/Gas 4 for about 50 minutes.

GRAINS AND PULSES

Mediterranean countries deserve thanks for the creation of risotto, focaccia, pizzas and pasta, and the many dishes based on dried pulses.

FOCACCIA

This is a flattish bread, originating from Genoa in Italy, made with flour, olive oil and salt. There are many variations, from many regions, including stuffed varieties, and versions topped with onions, olives or herbs.

25g/1oz fresh yeast
400g/14oz/3½ cups strong plain flour
10ml/2 tsp salt
75ml/5 tbsp olive oil
10ml/2 tsp coarse sea salt

MAKES 1 ROUND 25CM/10IN LOAF

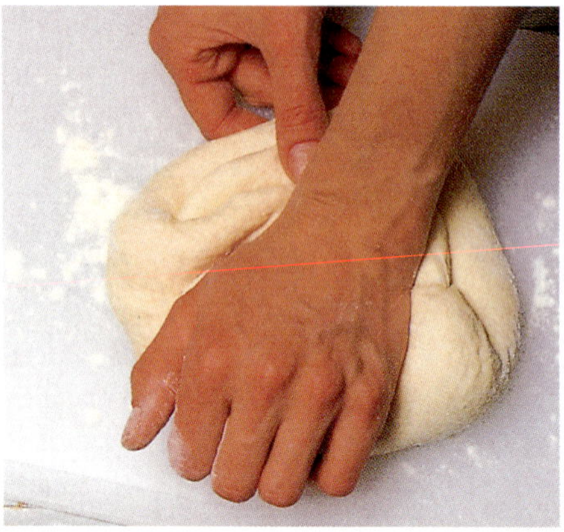

1 Dissolve the yeast in 120ml/4fl oz/½ cup warm water. Allow to stand for 10 minutes. Sift the flour into a large bowl, make a well in the centre, and add the yeast, salt and 30ml/2 tbsp oil. Mix in the flour and add more water to make a dough.

2 Turn out on to a floured surface and knead the dough for about 10 minutes, until smooth and elastic. Return to the bowl, cover with a cloth, and leave to rise in a warm place for 2–2½ hours until the dough has doubled in bulk.

3 Knock back the dough and knead again for a few minutes. Press into an oiled 25cm/10in tart tin, and cover with a damp cloth. Leave to rise for 30 minutes.

4 Preheat the oven to 200°C/400°F/Gas 6. Poke the dough all over with your fingers, to make little dimples in the surface. Pour the remaining oil over the dough, using a pastry brush to take it to the edges. Sprinkle with the salt.

5 Bake for 20–25 minutes, until the bread is a pale gold. Carefully remove from the tin and leave to cool on a rack. The bread is best eaten on the same day, but it also freezes very well.

ONION FOCACCIA

This pizza-like flat bread is characterized by its soft dimpled surface, sometimes dredged simply with coarse salt, or with onions, herbs or olives. It tastes delicious served warm with soups and stews.

675g/1½lb/6 cups strong plain flour
2.5ml/½ tsp salt
2.5ml/½ tsp caster sugar
15ml/1 tbsp easy-blend dried yeast
60ml/4 tbsp extra virgin olive oil
450ml/¾ pint/1⅞ cups hand-hot water

TO FINISH
2 red onions, thinly sliced
45ml/3 tbsp extra virgin olive oil
15ml/1 tbsp coarse salt

MAKES TWO 25CM/10IN LOAVES

1. Sift the flour, salt and sugar into a large bowl. Stir in the yeast, oil and water and mix to a dough using a round-bladed knife. (Add a little extra water if the dough is dry.)

2. Turn out on to a lightly floured surface and knead for about 10 minutes until smooth and elastic.

3. Put the dough in a clean, lightly oiled bowl and cover with clear film. Leave to rise in a warm place until doubled in bulk.

4. Place two 25cm/10in plain metal flan rings on baking sheets. Oil the insides of the rings and the baking sheets.

5. Preheat the oven to 200°C/400°F/Gas 6. Halve the dough and roll each piece to a 25cm/10in round. Press into the tins, cover with a dampened dish cloth and leave for 30 minutes to rise.

6. Make deep holes, about 2.5cm/1in apart, in the dough. Cover and leave for a further 20 minutes.

7. Scatter with the onions and drizzle over the oil. Sprinkle with the salt. then a little cold water, to stop a crust from forming.

8. Bake for about 25 minutes, sprinkling with water again during cooking. Cool on a wire rack.

SPANISH ONION AND ANCHOVY PIZZA

This pizza has flavours and ingredients brought to Spain by the Moors and still used today in many classic Spanish recipes.

400g/14oz/2½ cups strong plain flour
2.5ml/½ tsp salt
15g/½oz easy-blend dried yeast
120ml/4fl oz/½ cup olive oil
150ml/¼ pint/⅔ cup milk and water, in equal quantities, mixed together
3 large onions, thinly sliced
50g/2oz can anchovies, drained and roughly chopped
30ml/2 tbsp pine nuts
30ml/2 tbsp sultanas
5ml/1 tsp dried chilli flakes or powder
salt and ground black pepper

SERVES 6–8

1 Sift the flour and salt together into a large bowl. Stir in the yeast. Make a well in the centre, and add 60ml/4 tbsp of the olive oil, and a little of the milk and water. Bring the flour mixture and liquid together, gradually adding the remaining milk and water, until a dough is formed. Knead on a floured surface for about 10 minutes. Return to the bowl, cover with a cloth, and leave in a warm place to rise for about 1 hour.

2 Heat the remaining oil in a large frying pan, add the onions, and cook until soft. Preheat the oven to 240°C/475°F/Gas 9.

3 Knock back the dough, and roll out to a rectangle about 30 x 38cm/12 x 15in. Place on an oiled baking sheet. Cover with the onions. Scatter over the anchovies, pine nuts, sultanas and chilli flakes. Season. Bake for 10–15 minutes, until the edges are beginning to brown. Serve hot.

SUN-DRIED TOMATO BREAD

In the south of Italy, tomatoes are often dried off in the hot sun. They are then preserved in oil, or hung up in strings in the kitchen, to use in the winter. This recipe uses the former.

675g/1½lb/6 cups strong plain flour
10ml/2 tsp salt
25g/1oz/2 tbsp caster sugar
25g/1oz fresh yeast
400–475ml/14–16fl oz/1⅔–2 cups warm milk
15ml/1 tbsp tomato purée
75ml/5 tbsp oil from the jar of sun-dried tomatoes
75ml/5 tbsp extra virgin olive oil
75g/3oz/¾ cup drained sun-dried tomatoes, chopped
1 large onion, chopped

MAKES 4 SMALL LOAVES

1 Sift the flour, salt and sugar into a bowl, and make a well in the centre. Crumble the yeast, mix with 150ml/¼ pint/⅔ cup of the warm milk and add to the flour.

2 Mix the tomato purée into the remaining milk, until evenly blended, then add to the flour with the tomato oil and olive oil.

3 Gradually mix the flour into the liquid ingredients, until you have a dough. Turn out on to a floured surface, and knead for about 10 minutes, until smooth and elastic. Return to the clean bowl, cover with a cloth, and leave to rise in a warm place for about 2 hours.

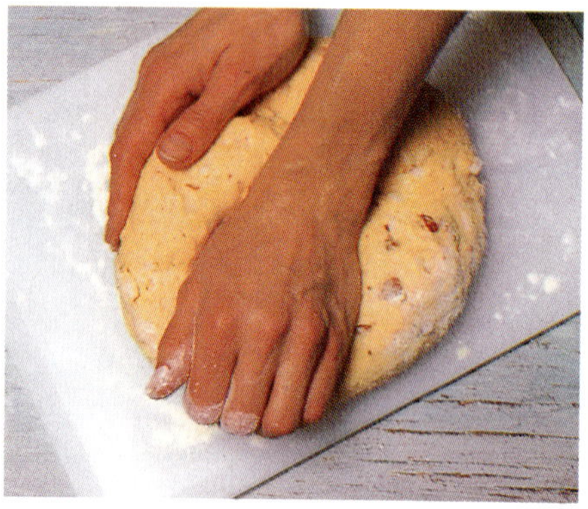

4 Knock the dough back, and add the tomatoes and onion. Knead until evenly distributed through the dough. Shape into four rounds and place on a greased baking sheet. Cover with a dish towel and leave to rise again for about 45 minutes.

5 Preheat the oven to 190°C/375°F/Gas 5. Bake the bread for 45 minutes, or until the loaves sound hollow when you tap them underneath with your fingers. Leave to cool on a wire rack. Eat warm, or toasted with grated mozzarella cheese on top.

COOK'S TIP
Use a pair of sharp kitchen scissors to cut up the sun-dried tomatoes.

RISOTTO ALLA MILANESE

Italian risottos have a distinctive creamy texture that is achieved by using arborio rice, a short grain rice which absorbs plenty of stock, but at the same time retains its texture. This risotto, scattered with cheese and gremolata, makes a delicious light meal or accompaniment to a meaty stew or casserole.

FOR THE GREMOLATA

2 garlic cloves, crushed
60ml/4 tbsp chopped fresh parsley
finely grated rind of 1 lemon

FOR THE RISOTTO

5ml/1 tsp (or 1 sachet) saffron strands
25g/1oz/2 tbsp butter
1 large onion, finely chopped
275g/10oz/1½ cups arborio (risotto) rice
150ml/¼ pint/⅔ cup dry white wine
1 litre/1¾ pints/4 cups chicken or vegetable stock
salt and ground black pepper
Parmesan cheese shavings

SERVES 4

1 To make the gremolata, mix together the garlic, parsley and lemon rind and reserve.

2 To make the risotto, put the saffron in a small bowl with 15ml/1 tbsp boiling water and leave to stand. Melt the butter in a heavy-based saucepan and gently fry the onion for 5 minutes.

3 Stir in the rice and cook for about 2 minutes until it becomes translucent. Add the wine and saffron mixture and cook for several minutes until the wine is absorbed.

4 Add 600ml/1 pint/2½ cups of the stock to the pan and simmer gently until the stock is absorbed, stirring frequently.

5 Gradually add more stock, a ladleful at a time, until the rice is tender. (The rice might be tender and creamy before you've added all the stock so add it slowly towards the end of the cooking time.)

6 Season the risotto with salt and pepper and transfer to a serving dish. Scatter lavishly with shavings of Parmesan cheese and the gremolata.

VARIATION

If preferred, stir plenty of grated Parmesan cheese into the risotto.

SPICED VEGETABLE COUSCOUS

Couscous, a cereal processed from semolina, is used throughout North Africa, mostly in Morocco, where it is served with meat, poultry and Moroccan vegetable stews or tagines.

45ml/3 tbsp vegetable oil
1 large onion, finely chopped
2 garlic cloves, crushed
15ml/1 tbsp tomato purée
2.5ml/½ tsp ground turmeric
2.5ml/½ tsp cayenne pepper
5ml/1 tsp ground coriander
5ml/1 tsp ground cumin
225g/8oz/1½ cups cauliflower florets
225g/8oz baby carrots, trimmed
1 red pepper, seeded and diced
4 beefsteak tomatoes
225g/8oz/1¾ cups courgettes, thickly sliced
400g/14oz can chick-peas, drained and rinsed
45ml/3 tbsp chopped fresh coriander
salt and ground black pepper
coriander sprigs, to garnish

FOR THE COUSCOUS

5ml/1 tsp salt
450g/1lb/2⅔ cups couscous
50g/2oz/2 tbsp butter

SERVES 6

1 Heat 30ml/2 tbsp of the oil in a large pan, add the onion and garlic, and cook until soft. Stir in the tomato purée, turmeric, cayenne, ground coriander and cumin. Cook, stirring, for 2 minutes.

2 Add the cauliflower, carrots and pepper, with enough water to come halfway up the vegetables. Bring to the boil, then lower the heat, cover and simmer for 10 minutes.

COOK'S TIP

Beefsteak tomatoes have excellent flavour and are ideal for this recipe, but you can substitute six ordinary tomatoes or two 400g/14oz cans chopped tomatoes.

3 Plunge the tomatoes into boiling water for 30 seconds, then refresh in cold water. Peel away the skins and chop. Add the sliced courgettes, chick-peas and tomatoes to the other vegetables and cook for a further 10 minutes. Stir in the fresh coriander and season with salt and pepper. Keep hot.

4 To cook the couscous, bring 475ml/16fl oz/2 cups water to the boil in a large saucepan. Add the remaining oil and the salt. Remove from the heat, and add the couscous, stirring. Allow to swell for 2 minutes, then add the butter, and heat through gently, stirring to separate the grains.

5 Turn the couscous out on to a warm serving dish, and spoon the vegetables on top, pouring over any liquid. Garnish and serve.

Hummus bi Tahina

Blending chick-peas with garlic and oil makes a surprisingly creamy purée that is delicious as part of a Turkish-style mezze, or as a dip with vegetables. Leftovers make a good sandwich filler.

150g/5oz/¾ cup dried chick-peas
juice of 2 lemons
2 garlic cloves, sliced
30ml/2 tbsp olive oil
pinch of cayenne pepper
150ml/¼ pint/⅔ cup tahini paste
salt and ground black pepper
extra olive oil and cayenne pepper for sprinkling
flat leaf parsley, to garnish

Serves 4–6

1. Put the chick-peas in a bowl with plenty of cold water and leave to soak overnight.

2. Drain the chick-peas and cover with fresh water in a saucepan. Bring to the boil and boil rapidly for 10 minutes. Reduce the heat and simmer gently for about 1 hour until soft. Drain.

3. Process the chick-peas in a food processor to a smooth purée. Add the lemon juice, garlic, olive oil, cayenne pepper and tahini and blend until creamy, scraping the mixture down from the sides of the bowl.

4. Season the purée with salt and pepper and transfer to a serving dish. Sprinkle with oil and cayenne pepper and serve garnished with a few parsley sprigs.

Cook's Tip

For convenience, canned chick-peas can be used instead. Allow two 400g/14oz cans and drain them thoroughly. Tahini paste can now be purchased from most supermarkets or health food shops.

FALAFEL

In North Africa these spicy fritters are made using dried broad beans, but chick-peas are much easier to buy. They are lovely served as a snack with garlicky yogurt or stuffed into warmed pitta bread.

150g/5oz/¾ cup dried chick-peas
1 large onion, roughly chopped
2 garlic cloves, roughly chopped
60ml/4 tbsp roughly chopped parsley
5ml/1 tsp cumin seeds, crushed
5ml/1 tsp coriander seeds, crushed
2.5ml/½ tsp baking powder
salt and ground black pepper
oil for deep frying
pitta bread, salad and yogurt, to serve

SERVES 4

1 Put the chick-peas in a bowl with plenty of cold water. Leave to soak overnight.

2 Drain the chick-peas and cover with water in a pan. Bring to the boil. Boil rapidly for 10 minutes. Reduce the heat and simmer for about 1 hour until soft. Drain.

3 Place in a food processor with the onion, garlic, parsley, cumin, coriander and baking powder. Add salt and pepper to taste. Process until the mixture forms a firm paste.

4 Shape the mixture into walnut-size balls and flatten them slightly. In a deep pan, heat 5cm/2in oil until a little of the mixture sizzles on the surface. Fry the falafel in batches until golden. Drain on kitchen paper and keep hot while frying the remainder. Serve warm in pitta bread, with salad and yogurt.

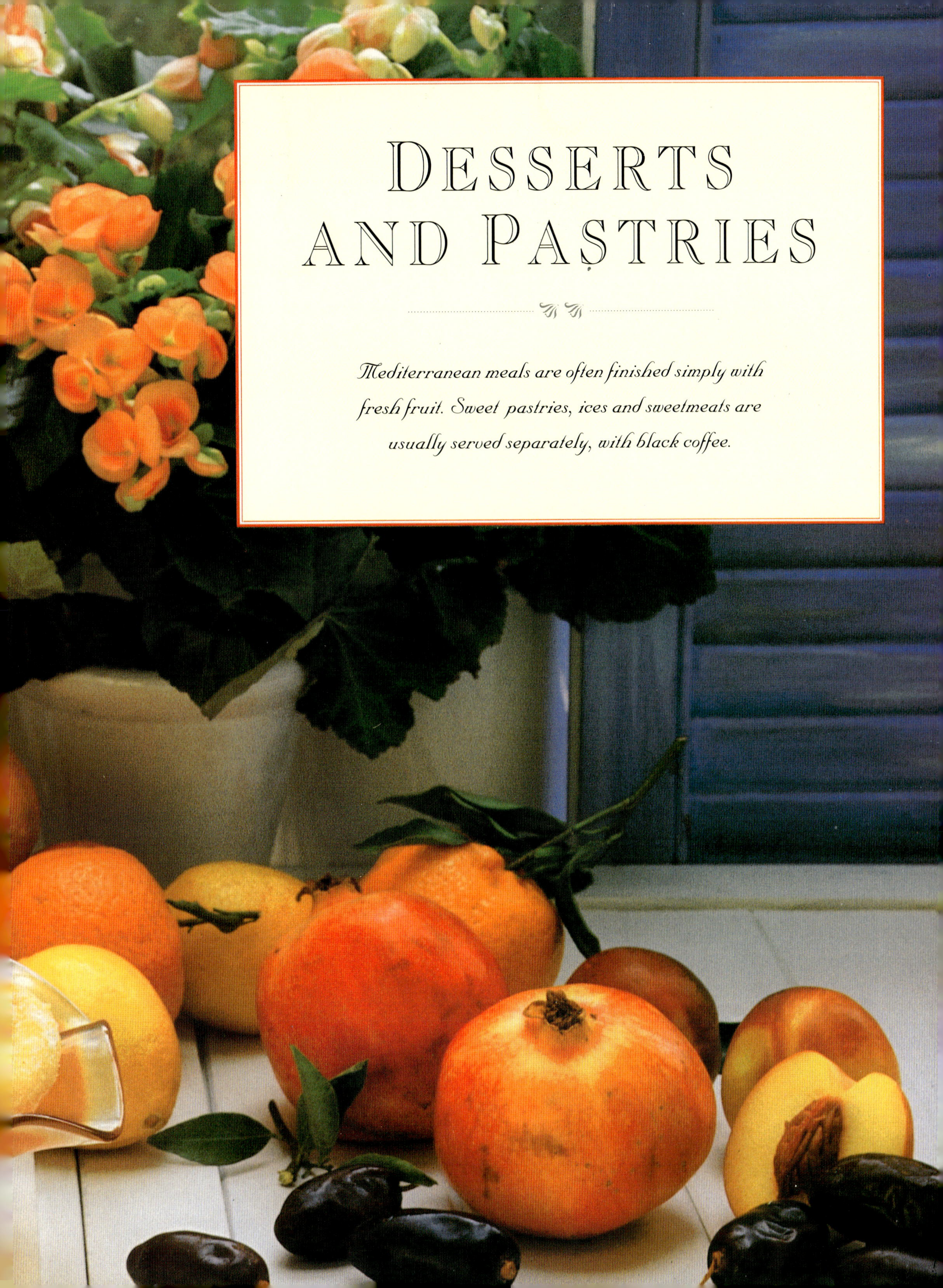

DESSERTS AND PASTRIES

Mediterranean meals are often finished simply with fresh fruit. Sweet pastries, ices and sweetmeats are usually served separately, with black coffee.

CHURROS

These Spanish doughnuts are commercially deep fried in huge coils and broken off into smaller lengths for selling. Serve this home-made version freshly cooked with hot chocolate or strong coffee.

200g/7oz/1¾ cups plain flour
1.5ml/¼ tsp salt
30ml/2 tbsp caster sugar
60ml/4 tbsp olive or sunflower oil
1 egg, beaten
caster sugar and ground cinnamon for dusting
oil for deep frying

MAKES 12–15

1 Sift the flour, salt and sugar on to a plate or piece of paper. Heat 250ml/8fl oz/1 cup water in a saucepan with the oil until it boils.

2 Tip in the flour mixture and beat with a wooden spoon until the mixture forms a stiff paste. Leave to cool for 2 minutes.

3 Gradually beat in the egg until smooth. Oil a large baking sheet. Sprinkle plenty of sugar on to a plate and stir in a little cinnamon.

4 Put the dough in a large piping bag fitted with a 1cm/½in plain piping nozzle. Pipe little coils or "s" shapes on to the baking sheet.

5 Heat 5cm/2in of oil in a large pan to 168°C/336°F or until a little dough sizzles on the surface.

6 Using an oiled fish slice, lower several of the piped shapes into the oil and cook for about 2 minutes until light golden.

7 Drain on kitchen paper then coat with the sugar and cinnamon mixture. Cook the remaining churros in the same way and serve immediately.

CHERRY CLAFOUTIS

When fresh cherries are in season this makes a deliciously simple dessert for any occasion. Serve warm with a little pouring cream.

675g/1½lb fresh cherries
50g/2oz/½ cup plain flour
pinch of salt
4 eggs, plus 2 egg yolks
115g/4oz/½ cup caster sugar
600ml/1 pint/2½ cups milk
50g/2oz/¼ cup melted butter
caster sugar for dusting

SERVES 6

1 Preheat the oven to 190°C/375°F/Gas 5. Lightly butter the base and sides of a shallow ovenproof dish. Stone the cherries and place in the dish.

2 Sift the flour and salt into a bowl. Add the eggs, egg yolks, sugar and a little of the milk and whisk to a smooth batter.

3 Gradually whisk in the rest of the milk and the rest of the butter, then strain the batter over the cherries. Bake for 40–50 minutes until golden and just set. Serve warm, dusted with caster sugar, if you like.

VARIATION

Use 2 x 425g/15oz cans stoned black cherries, thoroughly drained, if fresh cherries are not available. For a special dessert, add 45ml/3 tbsp kirsch to the batter.

STUFFED PEACHES WITH MASCARPONE CREAM

Mascarpone is a thick velvety Italian cream cheese, made from cow's milk. It is often used in desserts, or eaten with fresh fruit.

4 large peaches, halved and stoned
40g/1½oz amaretti biscuits, crumbled
30ml/2 tbsp ground almonds
45ml/3 tbsp sugar
15ml/1 tbsp cocoa powder
150ml/¼ pint/⅔ cup sweet wine
25g/1oz/2tbsp butter

For the mascarpone cream
30ml/2 tbsp caster sugar
3 egg yolks
15ml/1 tbsp sweet wine
225g/8oz/1 cup mascarpone cheese
150ml/¼ pint/⅔ cup double cream

Serves 4

1 Preheat the oven to 200°C/400°F/Gas 6. Using a teaspoon, scoop some of the flesh from the cavities in the peaches, to make a reasonable space for stuffing. Chop the scooped-out flesh.

2 Mix together the amaretti, ground almonds, sugar, cocoa and peach flesh. Add enough wine to make the mixture into a thick paste.

3 Place the peaches in a buttered ovenproof dish and fill them with the stuffing. Dot with the butter, then pour the remaining wine into the dish. Bake for 35 minutes.

4 To make the mascarpone cream, beat the sugar and egg yolks until thick and pale. Stir in the wine, then fold in the mascarpone. Whip the double cream to soft peaks and fold into the mixture. Remove the peaches from the oven and leave to cool. Serve at room temperature, with the mascarpone cream.

LEMON TART

This is one of the classic French desserts, and it is difficult to beat. A rich lemon curd, encased in crisp pastry. Crème fraîche is an optional accompaniment.

FOR THE PASTRY
225g/8oz/2 cups plain flour
115g/4oz/½ cup butter
30ml/2 tbsp icing sugar
1 egg
5ml/1 tsp vanilla essence

FOR THE FILLING
6 eggs, beaten
350g/12oz/1½ cups caster sugar
115g/4oz/½ cup unsalted butter
grated rind and juice of 4 lemons
icing sugar for dusting

SERVES 6

1 Preheat the oven to 200°C/400°F/Gas 6. Sift the flour into a bowl, add the butter, and work with your fingertips until the mixture resembles fine breadcrumbs. Stir in the icing sugar.

2 Add the egg, vanilla essence and a scant tablespoon of cold water, then work to a dough.

3 Roll the pastry out on a floured surface, and use to line a 23cm/9in tart tin. Line with foil or greaseproof paper and fill with dried beans or rice, or baking beans if you have them. Bake for 10 minutes.

4 To make the filling, put the eggs, sugar and butter into a pan, and stir over a low heat until the sugar has dissolved completely. Add the lemon rind and juice, and continue cooking, stirring all of the time, until the lemon curd has thickened slightly.

5 Pour the mixture into the pastry case. Bake for 20 minutes, until just set. Transfer the tart to a wire rack to cool. Dust with icing sugar just before serving.

GLAZED PRUNE TART

Generously glazed, creamy custard tarts are a pâtisserie favourite all over France. Plump prunes, heavily laced with brandy or kirsch, add a wonderful taste and texture to this deliciously sweet and creamy filling.

225g/8oz/1 cup ready-to-eat prunes
60ml/4 tbsp brandy or kirsch

FOR THE SWEET PASTRY
175g/6oz/1½ cups plain flour
pinch of salt
115g/4oz/½ cup unsalted butter
25g/1oz/2 tbsp caster sugar
2 egg yolks

FOR THE FILLING
150ml/¼ pint/⅔ cup double cream
150ml/¼ pint/⅔ cup milk
1 vanilla pod
3 eggs
50g/2oz/¼ cup caster sugar

TO FINISH
60ml/4 tbsp apricot jam
15ml/1 tbsp brandy or kirsch
icing sugar for dusting

SERVES 8

1 Put the prunes in a bowl with the brandy or kirsch and leave for about 4 hours until most of the liqueur has been absorbed.

2 To make the pastry, sift the flour and salt into a bowl. Add the butter, cut into small pieces, and rub in with the fingertips. Stir in the sugar and egg yolks and mix to a dough using a round-bladed knife.

3 Turn the dough out onto a lightly floured surface and knead to a smooth ball. Wrap closely and chill for 30 minutes.

4 Preheat the oven to 200°C/400°F/Gas 6. Roll out the pastry on a lightly floured surface and use to line a 24–25cm/9½–10in loose-based flan tin.

5 Line with greaseproof paper and fill with dried beans or rice, or baking beans if you have them. Bake for 15 minutes. Remove the beans and paper and bake for a further 5 minutes.

6 Arrange the prunes, evenly spaced, in the pastry case, reserving any liqueur left in the bowl.

7 For the filling, put the cream and milk in a saucepan with the vanilla pod and bring to the boil. Turn off the heat and leave the mixture to infuse for 15 minutes.

8 Whisk together the eggs and sugar in a bowl. Remove the vanilla pod from the cream and return the cream to the boil. Pour over the eggs and sugar, whisking to make a smooth custard.

9 Cool slightly then pour the custard over the prunes. Bake the tart for about 25 minutes until the filling is lightly set and turning golden around the edges.

10 Press the apricot jam through a sieve into a small pan. Add the liqueur and heat through gently. Use to glaze the tart. Serve warm or cold, dusted with icing sugar.

COOK'S TIP
The vanilla pod can be washed and dried, ready for using another time. Alternatively, use 5ml/1 tsp vanilla or almond essence.